[you] RiFe

[you] Ruined It For Everyone!

101 PEOPLE WHO SCREWED
THINGS UP FOR THE REST OF US

matthew vincent

Soft Skull Press
New York

Library of Congress Cataloging-in-Publication Data
Vincent, Matthew.
  [you] ruined it for everyone! : 101 people who screwed things up for the rest of us / Matthew Vincent.
     p. cm.
  Includes bibliographical references and index.
  ISBN 978-1-59376-288-9 (alk. paper)
1. Popular culture—Humor. 2. Popular culture–Miscellanea. I. Title.

PN6231.P635V56 2010
818'.602–dc22
2010019519

Cover design and interior design by Fluid Figment
www.fluidfigment.com

Typesetting by Neuwirth & Associates, Inc.
Printed in the United States of America

Soft Skull Press
An Imprint of Counterpoint LLC
1919 Fifth Street
Berkeley, CA 94710

www.softskull.com
www.counterpointpress.com

Distributed by Publishers Group West

10 9 8 7 6 5 4 3 2 1

for mélanie
+ téa

Contents

Introduction

How to Use This Book

Disclaimer

001 — Stella Liebeck
(For promoting ridiculous lawsuits)

002 — De Beers
(For making us spend two months' salary)

003 — Peter Travis
(For inventing Speedos)

004 — Anheuser-Busch
(For the first corporate-branded stadium)

005 — Muntadhar al-Zeidi
(For having bad aim)

006 — The U.S. Treasury and Mint
(For making America change)

007 — Abdulla Ahmed Ali
(For allowing only three ounces in planes)

008 — Tropicana
(For making O J NOT taste like oranges)

009 — Gordon Dancy
(For replacing paper with plastic)

010 — Ronald Clark O'Bryan
(For making us fear Halloween candy)

011 — Al Gore
(For telling us about global warming)

012 — George Vernon Hudson
(For inventing daylight saving time)

013 — Triskaidekaphobia
(For cutting out the thirteenth floor)

014 — Thomas Jefferson
(For the first U.S. political sex scandal)

015 — Ticketmaster
(For making a $20 ticket cost $32.50)

016 — Gillette
(For being too cutting-edge)

017 — Robert Ramon
(For making wine look cheap)

018 — Mary Kay Letourneau
(For gettin' it on with a thirteen-year-old)

019 — Sonny Bono and Michael Kennedy
(For future ski-helmet laws)

020 — McGraw-Hill
(For promoting the Y2K fear)

021 — Alcohol
(For being the devil's nectar)

022 — The inventor of plastic packaging
(For causing unnecessary ER visits)

023 — O.J. Simpson's (first) jury
(For letting a guilty man walk free)

024 — Guy standing up at a concert
(For ruining a good time)

025 — Richard Gere
(For making it a sin to own a gerbil)

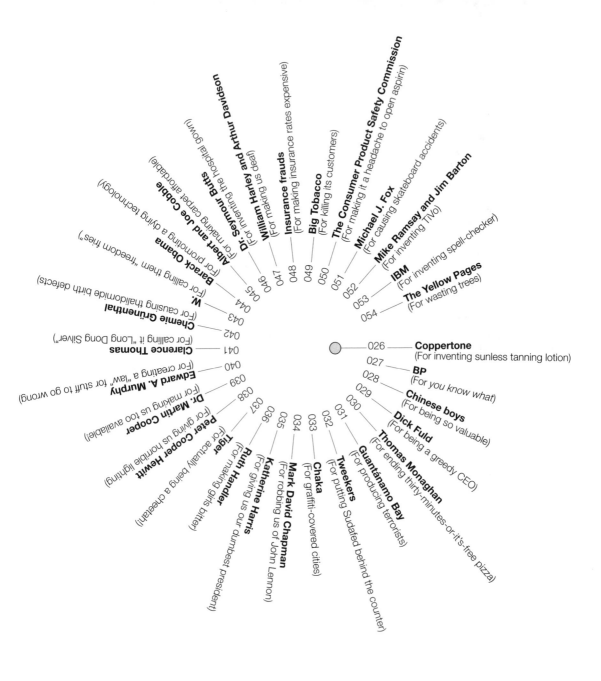

- **Coppertone** (For inventing sunless tanning lotion) — 026
- **BP** (For you know what) — 027
- **Chinese boys** (For being so valuable) — 028
- **Dick Fuld** (For being a greedy CEO) — 029
- **Thomas Monaghan** (For ending thirty-minutes-or-it's-free pizza) — 030
- **Guantánamo Bay** (For producing terrorists) — 031
- **Tweekers** (For putting Sudafed behind the counter) — 032
- **Chaka** (For graffiti-covered cities) — 033
- **Mark David Chapman** (For robbing us of John Lennon) — 034
- **Katherine Harris** (For giving us our dumbest president) — 035
- **Ruth Handler** (For making girls bitter) — 036
- **Tiger** (For actually being a cheetah!) — 037
- **Peter Cooper Hewitt** (For giving us horrible lighting) — 038
- **Dr. Martin Cooper** (For making us too available) — 039
- **Edward A. Murphy** (For creating a "law" for stuff to go wrong) — 040
- **Clarence Thomas** (For calling it "Long Dong Silver") — 041
- **Chemie Grünenthal** (For causing thalidomide birth defects) — 042
- **W.** (For calling them "freedom fries") — 043
- **Barack Obama** (For promoting a dying technology) — 044
- **Albert and Joe Cobble** (For inventing the hospital gown) — 045
- **Dr. Seymour Butts** (For making carpet affordable) — 046
- **William Harley and Arthur Davidson** (For making us deaf) — 047
- **Insurance frauds** (For making insurance rates expensive) — 048
- **Big Tobacco** (For killing its customers) — 049
- **The Consumer Product Safety Commission** (For making it a headache to open aspirin) — 050
- **Michael J. Fox** (For causing skateboard accidents) — 051
- **Mike Ramsay and Jim Barton** (For inventing TiVo) — 052
- **IBM** (For inventing spell-checker) — 053
- **The Yellow Pages** (For wasting trees) — 054

055 **Maurice Gatsonides** (For inventing photo traffic citations)

056 **Overprotective parents** (For ruining children)

057 **Jack Welch** (For security tag false alarms)

058 **Alex Rodriguez** (For teaching children it's okay to cheat)

059 **The automatic-flush toilet inventor** (For a cockamamie idea)

060 **Photoshop** (For tricking us into online dating)

061 **R. Stanton Avery** (For leaving a sticky residue)

062 **Germaphobes** (For ruining immune system development)

063 **The U.S. Department of Agriculture** (For inventing the four food groups)

064 **The imperial system of measurement** (For not going away)

065 **John DeLorean** (For producing only one car . . . sniff, sniff)

066 **Pope Siricius** (For being the devil in disguise)

067 **Ken Lay and Jeff Skilling** (For destroying Enron)

068 **Scott Boras and Drew Rosenhaus** (For ruining professional sports)

069 **Monica Lewinsky** (For sucking)

070 **Tyler Durden** (For questioning the safety of our cars)

071 **Sony's Betamax** (For starting format wars)

072 **Car alarm users** (For making a lot of noise)

073 **Asbestos companies** (For making our lungs biohazard sites)

074 **Dr. Robert Atkins** (For a stupid diet)

075 **Phil Gramm** (For legalizing deregulation)

076 **MLA Handbook** (For changing the spacing after a sentence)

077 **Blue star LSD warnings** (For being a stupid urban legend)

078 **The Food and Drug Administration** (For making healthy food unhealthy)

079 **Ron Popeil** (For coaxing people to buy hair in a can)

080 **James Mack Jr.** (For adding MORE worry to nursing homes)

081 **Barbra Streisand** (For crimped hair)

082 **Edward Seymour** (For inventing aerosol spray paint)

083 **Thomas Hamilton** (For causing the handgun ban in the U.K.)

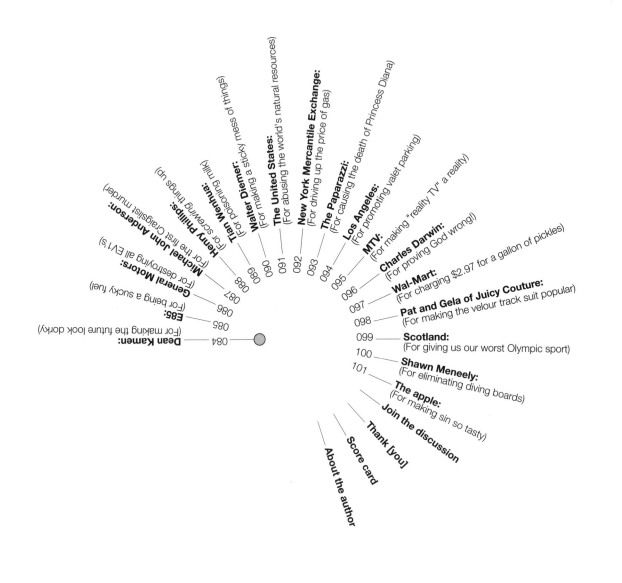

Walter Diemer:
(For making a sticky mess of things)

The United States:
(For abusing the world's natural resources)

New York Mercantile Exchange:
(For driving up the price of gas)

The Paparazzi:
(For causing the death of Princess Diana)

Los Angeles:
(For promoting valet parking)

MTV:
(For making "reality TV" a reality)

Charles Darwin:
(For proving God wrong!)

Wal-Mart:
(For charging $2.97 for a gallon of pickles)

Pat and Gela of Juicy Couture:
(For making the velour track suit popular)

Scotland:
(For giving us our worst Olympic sport)

Shawn Meneely:
(For eliminating diving boards)

The apple:
(For making sin so tasty)

Join the discussion

Thank [you]

Score card

About the author

Tian Wenhua:
(For poisoning milk)

Henry Phillips:
(For screwing things up)

Michael John Anderson:
(For the first Craigslist murder)

General Motors:
(For destroying all EV1's)

E85:
(For being a sucky fuel)

Dean Kamen:
(For making the future look dorky)

090
091
092
093
094
095
096
097
098
099
100
101
089
088
087
086
085
084

INTRODUCTION

Ever wonder who is responsible for everything that sucks? Well, I have, and this book is the result. It contains what are, in my opinion, 101 of the most egregious RIFEs—[people who] Ruined It For Everyone.

So sit back, relax, and get ready to point some fingers!

HOW TO USE THIS BOOK

This is an icon for the **RIFEr**.

[you] RIFE!
This is how [they] ruined it.

This says **"FACTS,"** but it's mostly just my biased opinion.

That is the case number.
They are in random order, I think.

This is the person (or entity) who **Ruined It For Everyone!**

This is what said person or entity is responsible for ruining.

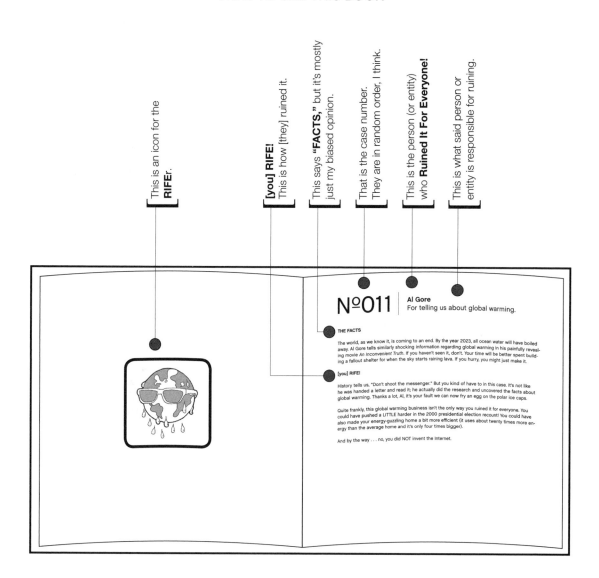

№011 Al Gore
For telling us about global warming.

THE FACTS

The world, as we know it, is coming to an end. By the year 2023, all ocean water will have boiled away. Al Gore tells similarly shocking information regarding global warming in his painfully revealing movie *An Inconvenient Truth*. If you haven't seen it, don't. Your time will be better spent building a fallout shelter for when the sky starts raining lava. If you hurry, you might just make it.

[you] RIFE!

History tells us, "Don't shoot the messenger." But you kind of have to in this case. It's not like he was handed a letter and read it; he actually did the research and uncovered the facts about global warming. Thanks a lot, Al, it's your fault we can now fry an egg on the polar ice caps.

Quite frankly, this global warming business isn't the only way you ruined it for everyone. You could have pushed a LITTLE harder in the 2000 presidential election recount! You could have also made your energy-guzzling home a bit more efficient (it uses about twenty times more energy than the average home and it's only four times bigger).

And by the way . . . no, you did NOT invent the Internet.

DISCLAIMER

Oh—this must be the part where the author wants to protect his ass. In a word, YEP. Did you just skip over that last page? It was really important and I must reiterate—the "FACTS" section of each RIFE is NOT necessarily factual. To the best of my knowledge it is true, but I didn't have the time or the resources to physically ask the people/companies mentioned in this book if every detail is true and legit. I Googled it. And believe it or not, there might be some untrue information available on the Internet. But at least I can proudly say that I did not step foot in one single library. And let's face it—some of the "FACTS" are lies told by me just to get a laugh. So, with that said, if you want to sue someone, sue Google—I'm sure they can spare the cash.

[you] RiFe

[you] Ruined It For Everyone!

№ 001

Stella Liebeck
For promoting ridiculous lawsuits.

THE FACTS

What paved the way for ridiculous lawsuits? In the last few decades, there has been a spike in lawsuits won by people who have blamed others for their own stupidity and ignorance. Ms. Liebeck may not have been the first to start the trend, but she certainly wins the blue ribbon.

In 1992, Stella Liebeck's grandson took her to a McDonald's drive-thru for a cup of coffee. After the purchase, they pulled over so Stella could add some cream and sugar. As the car sat motionless, she removed the cup's lid and clumsily spilled scalding hot coffee on her legs. This accident resulted in third-degree burns on 6 percent of her body. (Take note, she spilled it on herself. A Mickey Dee's employee did NOT drop it on her lap, nor did one vindictively throw the java in her face. It was just a simple, self-induced mistake.) After the incident, Ms. Liebeck sought $20,000 for pain and suffering. McDonald's refused to settle out of court (which ended up being a rather expensive mistake), and a jury awarded Ms. Liebeck $2.9 million.

[you] RIFE!

Why the hell is an eighty-one-year-old meddling with blisteringly hot coffee over her lap in a vehicle anyway? Did she forget what Dirty Harry said? Stella, "Man's got to know his limitations." This applies to grannies too! Now don't get me wrong, I love my Gram-Gram, and I'd certainly be laying the smack down if I caught someone messin' with her. But . . . she's old. She spills stuff all the time. It's expected. And McDonald's needs to share the blame too. Next time, don't use Grimace and the Hamburglar as legal counsel. Send a company-wide MEMO: *Juries tend to side with sweet old ladies in a BIG way!*

So thank you all, because this helped pave the way for anyone to sue anyone just for being a jackass. What happened next? Here you go: A guy sued Michael Jordan for looking like him. A family sued Honda because their daughter couldn't remove a seat belt while underwater and drunk. A woman sued Wendy's for finding a finger in her soup, which she planted herself. A guy sued a strip club because a dancer gave him whiplash. A family sued Oliver Stone because his movie inspired a woman's crime spree. A man sued a dry cleaner for $65 million because they lost his pants. I rest my case . . .

De Beers
For making us spend two months' salary.

THE FACTS

If you truly loved your girlfriend, you would spend at least two months' salary for her diamond engagement ring. If you find yourself asking, "Is that before or after taxes?", then you may also be wondering who came up with this bullshit. It was De Beers. The company also came up with "diamonds are forever" and "diamonds are a girl's best friend." It's the reason we associate a diamond solitaire with poppin' the question. De Beers started this marketing campaign in the 1930s and is still bamboozling us with this sparkly razzle-dazzle nonsense.

Everyone knows these diamond companies are shady, greedy, and sneaky. Just watch ten minutes of the movie *Blood Diamond* and you'll see. De Beers also keeps the price of diamonds high by controlling supply and demand. Try to forget about all that for a second, and focus on the question "Do you really NEED a diamond to propose?"

[you] RIFE!

Congratulations, De Beers, you convinced everyone that a diamond is mandatory when a guy gets down on one knee. You also made everyone think there is a direct correlation between the size of a diamond and the quality of love and devotion. Wake up, America! (Since you are, indeed, the world's largest diamond consumer.) You have been DUPED. Who says you have to buy a diamond ring for an engagement? Your girlfriend? No, the diamond industry tricks people with its exceptional marketing ploys. And we fall for it. De Beers claims you should spend about two months' salary. Since the typical American male makes about $36,000 a year, that means the average Joe owes his woman about $6,000 of sparkly (and tries his best to comply). More than 80 percent of American brides receive diamond engagement rings. Take note, about 95 percent of the U.S. population has sex before marriage. This means that most people refuse to obey God and the church regarding premarital sex, but they will listen to De Beers about the six grand.

Think, people, THINK! Spend your money on a great honeymoon or start a trust fund for your unborn child's education. Or maybe spend it on counseling before your marriage ends in divorce! Remember, a diamond is just a rock someone found in the ground. It takes more than digging in the dirt to make a marriage work.

№ 003 | Peter Travis
For inventing Speedos.

THE FACTS

Peter Travis was many things: a designer, sculptor, ceramist, kite-maker, and teacher. But the Australian is most famous for bringing millions of unwanted winces of disgust to the faces of people after seeing repulsive men wearing Speedos. This phenomenon is undeniably awful.

Don't get me wrong—the Speedo does have its place. It is, after all, very functional swimwear. It has low resistance for swimming competitions, it doesn't restrict movement while diving, and it can even lend itself to a bodybuilding competition (although that last point is highly debatable).

[you] RIFE!

Ah, the beach . . . a tranquil environment of warmth, soft breezes, and the calming effects of water. Picture yourself in sunny Florida lying on a blanket, about to apply some tanning lotion. Suddenly, you see something troubling. And like a needle scratching across a record, a hairy old guy struts right before your eyes sporting a banana hammock. Apparently someone forgot to remind him that he is not in Europe. Quite frankly, there is nothing more revolting than this phenomenon.

Finally, we know the wanker responsible for Speedos. Let's face it, Peter, the world could have done without this invention. It just makes everyone feel gross. Unfortunately, most of us were forced to wear Speedos while swimming in middle school gym class. Teachers told us we had to wear the uncomfortable trunks so everyone would look the same. But let me tell you, there is nothing "the same" about preteens when it comes to scrotal development. I blame Mr. Travis for the agonizingly embarrassing trauma of a late bloomer.

So take note: If you are a European man visiting American beaches or pools, we do not want to see your ass crack or your bulge, and we certainly DO NOT want to see your pubes. So stop it, and get some board shorts.

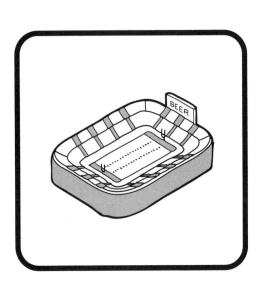

№004

Anheuser-Busch
For the first corporate-branded stadium.

THE FACTS

In 1953, Anheuser-Busch purchased the St. Louis Cardinals baseball franchise, along with its stadium, Sportsman Park. That same year, the brewers asked if they could rename the park, hoping to have "Budweiser" plastered on the stadium walls. However, the league president, Ford C. Frick, thought, ironically, that beer should not be associated with baseball, and said no. But he did allow the stadium to be named Busch Stadium, after the owner's name. So, under the influence of the president's support, Anheuser-Busch quickly, and deviously, started brewing a brand called Busch Bavarian Beer, later to be called Busch and Busch Light. And there you have it: the first stadium sponsorship was fermented.

[you] RIFE!

Today, the sobering truth is that nearly every stadium, arena, amphitheater, coliseum, concert hall, skating rink, and Little League field has been renamed by corporate sponsorship. I guess tradition and fond memories don't pay for today's overpriced, steroid-pumped athletes.

Now don't get me wrong—Busch is an okay beer. It isn't the best brew around, but I certainly don't turn it down when it's offered. In fact, most of what I have forgotten in college can be attributed to the affordability of Busch Light. But brewing a halfway decent cold one doesn't give Anheuser-Busch the right to sell out baseball's history.

And if a stadium name must be changed, at least make it cool. Here are some particularly sucky ones: Pizza Hut Park, Gaylord Entertainment Center, Heinz Field, Amway Arena, Minute Maid Park (take note of the improvement—it was previously named Enron Field), Dick's Sporting Goods Park, Lucas Oil Stadium, and Jobing.com Arena. Come on!

So the next time you "root, root, root" for the home team, don't forget that Anheuser-Busch stole the stadium's honor and respect and left you sitting in a giant ad campaign.

№005

Muntadhar al-Zeidi
For having bad aim.

THE FACTS

Austin Powers once asked, "Who throws a shoe? Honestly?" Well, the answer to that question, besides Dr. Evil's sidekick, Random Task, is a man I'm sure you have heard of—Muntadhar al-Zeidi.

In 2008, at a press conference in Iraq, President George W. Bush had to dodge two shoes swiftly thrown at him. His footwear-flinging attacker was Iraqi journalist Muntadhar al-Zeidi. Shoe-hurling is a grave insult in Arab culture. Zeidi was trying to show his disgust toward Bush's invasion of Iraq. Muntadhar, who had no prior criminal record, was sentenced to three years. Given the harmless nature of the crime (since nobody died from the shoe-icide), his sentence was reduced to one year after an appeal.

Muntadhar was considered a hero in many nations. A Saudi Arabian businessman offered him $10 million for one of his shoes. Also, as a result of the "shoe-ing," Turkish shoemaker Ramazan Baydan says his company, Baydan Shoes, had to employ one hundred additional workers to meet the extra demand customers who wanted to buy the same type of shoe thrown at the hated U.S. president.

[you] RIFE!

How did this sneaker-slinger ruin it for everyone? By MISSING, of course!

President Bush is an easy target to poke fun at, but, unfortunately for Muntadhar, a difficult one to hit with a shoe. In response, Bush did the only thing he could: He shrugged off the barely harmful act. However, if Bush were smart, he would have requested that the loafer-launcher be pardoned for freedom of speech (since Iraq is now a democracy, thanks to the U.S. invasion).

Don't give up, Muntadhar. Remember: Practice makes perfect!

The U.S. Treasury and Mint
For making America change.

THE FACTS

If a penny saved is a penny earned, then a penny made is a taxpayer played! Allow me to elaborate . . . actually, let's let the United States Mint director's cost analysis explain:

- Cost to mint a penny: 1.26 cents
- Cost to mint a nickel: 7.7 cents
- Cost to make a dollar coin: 16 cents
- Cost to make a dollar bill: 4.2 cents

[you] RIFE!

In case you need it spelled out for you, it costs MORE to mint the penny and the nickel than the coins' actual worth. And, if you forgot fourth-grade American history, your taxes pay for minting. Does this upset you? Well, now you finally have a good reason to smash that piggy bank!

That stupid annoying little penny . . . it and everything below the quarter needs to go away. Let's start dissolving as many as we can in bottles of Coke. And besides, except for buying a hotdog at the ball game, who the hell uses cash anymore? The U.S. Mint says 33 percent of all transactions use cash. That seems a bit high. The mint must be including all of Washington's untraceable private escort transactions in its statistics.

Anyway, if you haven't already, start lobbying your congressman and the March of Dimes. And be sure to max out your credit as often as possible to deter coin usage. I am sure we will experience some resistance from the bleeding hearts and conservatives. But don't worry—just tell them we can still use coins for circuit breakers and weddings, instead of throwing rice. Rice does kill birds, you know. And the next time you see Obama, tell him to fight for NO CHANGE!

A side note: Someone please tell the $1 bill to wipe that smirk off its face, because it only has a life expectancy of twenty-one months. So it can go away too. In fact, if it were replaced with the $1 coin, taxpayers would save over $500 million per year, since coins last at least thirty years!

I wonder how long it takes a dollar to dissolve in Coca-Cola.

Nº007

Abdulla Ahmed Ali
For allowing only three ounces in planes.

THE FACTS

Abdulla Ahmed Ali was one of the British Islamists arrested in connection with the 2006 transatlantic aircraft terrorist plot in the United Kingdom. He was the apparent mastermind of a terror cell that plotted to blow up airliners using liquid bombs disguised in drink bottles. Twenty-four men were arrested in Britain, but only three men, Abdulla Ahmed Ali, Assad Sarwar, and Tanvir Hussain, were convicted of conspiring to commit mass murder.

More than a thousand flights were canceled in the aftermath, and many countries imposed tight restrictions on carry-on baggage for several weeks. To this day, all travelers are still restricted to bottles that hold only about a thimbleful of liquid.

[you] RIFE!

Due to the liquid bomb plot, we are only allowed to take three-ounce bottles on a plane. Not to mention the much more enjoyable chaos of going through a "heightened security" screening. I comply with these laws, but it's such a nuisance. Air travel is no longer an adventure; it's a hassle.

Let me take you back down memory lane . . . I remember going to the airport to drop my dad off for a business trip. Back then, we would stay at the gate, our noses pressed to the window, fogging up the glass, until his plane was nothing more than a speck in the sky. Even when we picked him up, we would go inside an hour early and giddily wait for his face to pop through the long human tube. However, those days are gone. Wake up from nostalgia, everybody: We are in a new era of "safety." Nowadays a drop-off is nothing more than a kick to the curb, and a pickup usually involves a cab ride. I really feel we lost something.

But there is nothing we can do about it now, so wipe that tear from your eye, because TSA might not let you carry it on.

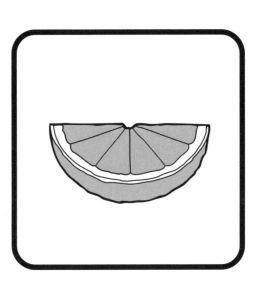

THE FACTS

Ever notice that your local grocery store will sometimes have an incredible deal on strawberries? I am sure you already know why; it's because they are "in season." It was the best time to harvest a few weeks prior to the sale and the grocery store overbought, so they try to force-feed you with crazy-good deals. Well, all fruits and vegetables have an optimal harvesting season. The popular, and best-tasting, Valencia oranges grown in Florida are certainly not exempt from this rule. The primary picking time for this tasty citrus fruit is from March until June. So how do Tropicana and other orange juice companies make consistent-tasting juice year round? Well, they cheat by using "flavor packs." These flavor "enhancers" are made by flavor and fragrance companies, the same ones that make your perfume, soap, and deodorant smell good. You will not find these ingredients printed on the juice box, since they use orange essence and oil and are technically part of the orange. However, chemically altered orange peel is certainly NOT nature intended juice to be made of.

More than six hundred and twenty million gallons of orange juice are sold every year in the U.S. Unfortunately, 99 percent of it does not taste like real squeezed oranges. If you were drinking "real" orange juice, the flavor would vary with the seasons (and you would also get the benefits of 30 percent more vitamins).

[you] RIFE!

In the eighties, Tropicana ruined it by convincing everyone that "not from concentrate" meant "fresher." And then it changed from "concentrate" to "pasteurized," which was another marketing ploy. "Pasteurized" simply sounds even more fresh, but, ironically, it doesn't make it fresher; it only means the liquid content has not been removed. Here's what they do: They rapidly heat the juice, remove the oxygen, and then store it. This process strips the juice of most of its flavor. After that, the juice is stored for up to a year before fake "flavor" is added, and then the juice is sold.

Do yourself a favor—take a Valencia orange, squeeze it, and then do a taste test with store-bought, pasteurized, not-from-concentrate orange juice. Your taste buds will be angry. So don't forget to drink your morning dose of vitamin C. And remember, the "C" stands for Conned!

№009

Gordon Dancy
For replacing paper with plastic.

THE FACTS

Indirectly, Mr. Dancy is responsible for the question "Will that be paper or plastic?" In the late 1970s, Gordon Dancy invented the plastic grocery bag for good reasons. At the time, people were concerned about saving trees. As in most circumstances, fixing one problem inevitably created another. Unfortunately, this quick fix was NOT thought through:

- Plastic bags are not biodegradable, and less than 5 percent are recycled.
- Americans throw away twelve thousand plastic bags per second.
- U.S. consumers use one hundred billion plastic bags each year, which equals twelve million barrels of oil.

This doesn't mean choosing paper is the solution. Both—paper and plastic—emit harmful gases during production. Paper weighs more and, in turn, requires more fuel in its nationwide delivery. And only about 20 percent of paper bags are actually recycled.

Is "Reduce, Reuse, Recycle" the answer? Recycling is great, but it encourages overconsumption. Reusing is paramount. And, if you are among the 65 percent of Americans who are overweight, give "reducing" a try too.

[you] RIFE!

Gordon, you really ruined it for everyone. Not only are plastic bags unsightly trash blowing through our neighborhoods, they have been proven detrimental to our environment and will NEVER biodegrade.

BTW, the correct answer to the "paper or plastic" question is: NEITHER! In case you missed the memo, the best thing is to carry a reusable bag. They sell these bags at ALL grocery stores for cheap, so buy some. Or, if you want to splurge, get some cool ones at www.envirosax.com. They look cool, scrunch down to about nothing, hold tons of swag, and last forever. Store them in your car or carry them with you and use them.

Ronald Clark O'Bryan
For making us fear Halloween candy.

THE FACTS

Every year, many rumors and myths about candy tampering and poisoning during Halloween time resurface. The delicious dark holiday has been plagued by worries of candy contamination for decades. Parents fear that some madman will poison and distribute candy to unsuspecting boys and girls during their yearly trick-or-treating. There most certainly have been some scares, as well as false accusations. However, rest assured, there have been no "true" cases of random Halloween poisoning.

Nonetheless, someone has used the myth to try to get away with murder . . .

[you] RIFE!

Okay, so Ronald O'Bryan did not invent the urban legend, but we have to blame someone, and he is about as nasty as someone can get. Long story short, he poisoned his own son with cyanide-laced Pixy Stix and blamed it on an aimless Halloween treat-giver. It turns out O'Bryan was just trying to collect on a large insurance policy he took out on the poor kid. He was found guilty and put to death, appropriately, by lethal injection.

Murder is one thing. Murdering a child is another. But putting the hit on your OWN son? Jokes fail me in this instance.

Another young boy, five years old, supposedly ate cruel counterfeit confections on All Hallows' Eve. But it turned out that story was just a cover-up. He accidentally poisoned himself with his uncle's all-too-accessible heroin stash. To throw off the police, the family sprinkled the drug on some candy after the child died. This brings the tally up to zero random psychos giving out tainted goodies on the frightful holiday. Which, statistically speaking, actually makes it safer to take candy from a stranger than from your own family. Nevertheless, parents still spend countless hours checking the safety of their kids' sweet stash every year for apparently no reason. Some even go to the airport to get the candy X-rayed. It has all been fueled by rumors, assumptions, and assholes like Ronald Clark O'Bryan.

№ 011

Al Gore
For telling us about global warming.

THE FACTS

The world as we know it is coming to an end. By the year 2023, all ocean water will have boiled away. Al Gore tells similarly shocking information regarding global warming in his painfully revealing movie *An Inconvenient Truth*. If you haven't seen it, don't. Your time will be better spent building a fallout shelter for when the sky starts raining lava. If you hurry, you might just make it.

[you] RIFE!

History tells us, "Don't shoot the messenger." But you kind of have to in this case. It's not like he was handed a letter and read it; he actually did the research and uncovered the facts about global warming. Thanks a lot, Al; it's your fault we can now fry an egg on the polar ice caps.

Quite frankly, this global warming business isn't the only way you ruined it for everyone. You could have pushed a LITTLE harder in the 2000 presidential election recount! You could have also made your energy-guzzling home a bit more efficient (it uses about twenty times more energy than the average home and it's only four times bigger).

And by the way . . . no, you did NOT invent the Internet.

George Vernon Hudson
For inventing daylight saving time.

THE FACTS

Time—a good magazine and a great Pink Floyd song . . . But let's get back to George Vernon Hudson and his role in daylight saving time. He first proposed the concept in 1895 in New Zealand. He felt having more daylight in the summer evenings would better our quality of life. But you can Google more about him in the fall since you won't know what to do with that extra hour you'll gain. You'll find he's the reason we have to reset our clocks and have more traffic accidents in the weeks after the time change.

There's always so much fuss and flurry about this topic. Should we do it? Should we not? Are we saving energy or just causing headaches? And what about the poor farmers and school buses? I think it's time for action!

[you] RIFE!

Do we really need daylight anyway? Let's just get rid of it altogether. I'll bet Seattle and New York wouldn't even notice the difference! We'll just put up football stadium lights everywhere and control the day with a flip of the switch! It'll be great! Then we wouldn't be confined to this pesky twenty-four-hour day. We really need thirty-six-hour days anyway. Then we could work fourteen hours, spend much more time with our families, and get a couple extra hours of sleep every night! AND it would cut the ageing process in HALF! It's genius! The only downside? Playtex will have to update to a thirty-hour bra.

Okay, here's how we'll do it—we need to fill up the atmosphere with smoke to eradicate the sunlight. If we legalized marijuana and started six more wildfires in California every year, that should do the trick. Then we'll have AM, PM, and MM—the "MM," of course, stands for "much more." It's gonna be great: No sunlight means less skin cancer, more time, and NO MORE spring-forward/fall-backward bullshit. We'll just let the little hand of our clocks have another go-round every day. Just think, your microwave will always read the correct time! Serenity now.

№ 013 | Triskaidekaphobia (fearing the number 13)
For cutting out the thirteenth floor.

THE FACTS

There are many superstitions in modern civilization. We have black cats to watch out for, ladders to avoid walking under, umbrellas we pray won't open indoors, and mirrors we are cautious not to break. But come on . . . picking on a poor little prime number seems like a bit much. Thirteen didn't do anything wrong. It wasn't bothering anyone when it sat happy and cozy between its little sis and big bro, twelve and fourteen. Then, one day, they stopped putting a thirteenth floor in all high-rise building WTF? How would you feel if someone took out your thirteenth vertebra? Paralyzed, that's how. Let's grow up and put that thirteenth button back in elevators.

[you] RIFE!

Your superstitions are ruining it for everyone *and* yourself. Get over your phobia—and enjoy thirteen things that are great about the number 13:

    I. There are thirteen new moons in a year. That's pretty good, right?

    II. Women have thirteen chances to get pregnant each year.

    III. There were thirteen original colonies in the United States. You like freedom, don't you?

    IV. Thirteen years old is the start of manhood. There's nothing unlucky about getting lucky.

    V. Dan Marino wore No. 13. Remember, Dan's the man.

    VI. Thirteen doughnuts are in a baker's dozen; twelve to a dozen is just so "carton of eggs."

    VII. The top-rated album of all time, *Sgt. Pepper's Lonely Hearts Club Band*, has thirteen songs.

    VIII. Thirteen people attended the Last Supper. Twelve's company, but thirteen's a da Vinci painting.

    IX. The PG-13 rating. You can see some nudity AND hear the F-bomb in a movie.

    X. Michael Jordan's shoe size is 13. Not exactly bad fortune there!

    XI. Aluminum is the most abundant metal in the earth's crust and it's No. 13 on the periodic table.

    XII. On the U.S. dollar bill, there are thirteen levels on the pyramid, thirteen arrows, thirteen stars, thirteen leaves, and thirteen olives. Is it no longer lucky to win a million of them?

    XIII. Last but not least, someone's mom's birthday was on Friday the 13th. And moms are good.

Now that you're convinced the number 13 is no longer bad, here's a few hotels with a thirteenth floor for you to visit: Embassy Suites in Tampa, Florida; the International Palace Hotel in Recife, Brazil; and the Sè Hotel in San Diego, California. (I am sure the word "die" found in "San Diego" is just a coincidence.)

№014

Thomas Jefferson
For the first U.S. political sex scandal.

THE FACTS

Thomas Jefferson was the third president of the United States (1801–1809). He was the main author of the Declaration of Independence, and he helped facilitate the Louisiana Purchase and commissioned the Lewis and Clark expedition. Arguably, he is one of the greatest U.S. presidents, and a founding father of the United States of America. Despite all of his achievements, the guy just couldn't keep his dick in his pants.

As it turns out, Jefferson was accused of seducing a close friend's wife. And he had an affair with the very married Maria Cosway. He also had a forty-year relationship with his wife's half-sister, a slave named Sally Hemmings. They had six children together.

[you] RIFE!

Jefferson was the John Holmes of the American political sexual revolution. He paved the way for hundreds of political sex scandals throughout U.S. history. He opened the floodgates to presidential knee pads, Long Dong Silvers, madam clients, underage male pages, bastard births, restroom solicitations, parked car rendezvouses, and the mysterious deaths of countless mistresses. Thanks again!

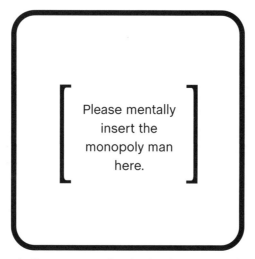

[Please mentally insert the monopoly man here.]

Lack of image courtesy of Hasbro for refusing usage rights.

Nº015

Ticketmaster
For making a $20 ticket cost $32.50.

THE FACTS

Ticketmaster is a ticket sales and distribution company based in West Hollywood, California. If you have never heard of it, you should really get out of the house more often. It's the company that sells almost all concert and sporting event tickets. The company is ridiculed for its outrageous service charges and has been accused, several times, of operating as a monopoly. However, Ticketmaster simply acts as an agent that sells the tickets its clients make available. So it's impossible to charge Ticketmaster as an illegal monopoly because they are a third-party entity. But no matter how you look at it, Ticketmaster still sucks.

[you] RIFE!

Shame on you, Ticketmaster. Your greed has made nearly every concertgoer curse your name for bankrupting him. Your ridiculous charges nearly parallel the bands' revenues. You are well hated and will undoubtedly fall at one point. And when you do, rest assured that we, the fans, will be there to kick ticket stubs in your face.

Shame on you, venues. You accept millions from Ticketmaster, allowing the company to have exclusive ticket-selling rights. You are the reason Ticketmaster can indiscriminately jack up its prices in the first place. Instead of making ticket sales a competitive business, you made it a virtual monopoly. Don't you get enough revenue from corporate sponsorship anyway (see RIFE Nº004)? You too have sold your souls to the devil.

Shame on the fans. We buy the tickets. We should rise up and boycott these overpriced events! But who am I kidding? That's never gonna happen. And besides, a picket line would just look like a ticket line anyway.

Shame on Pearl Jam too. You were so close to winning a lawsuit against Ticketmaster. Shame on you for giving up. Get better lawyers and sue them again. Forget the venues and start playing in back-yards. Then you'd be cool again.

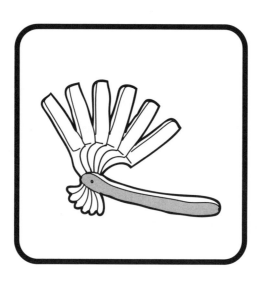

Nº016 | **Gillette**
For being too cutting-edge.

THE FACTS

Technology is great. Just look at all of the achievements and advancements you use in your daily life. Things seem to get faster, smaller, and smarter before you can fully sign your name on the service contract—it's crazy. But some things just DON'T need improvement. For example, Gillette now has a six-blade razor! SIX! It should come with tourniquet instructions and a panic button directly linked to 911 in case you slice any major arteries.

Hair always seems to grow in places we just don't want it to. So people will try anything; they will cut, pluck, tweeze, Nair, wax, zap, and laser. But nothing seems to be as reliable as shaving. So we strive for a good close shave, but we don't need six blades. It's not like we are using Windex and a squeegee for aftershave.

[you] RIFE!

When I was five, I wanted to be like my dad. And why not? He was my hero—and my hero shaved. One morning, my peach-fuzz-covered mug must've felt a bit too scruffy. So I lathered up all by myself. Not only was I disappointed at the non–Cool Whip flavor of the shaving cream, but I also gashed my ear and started bawling. My hero quickly came to my rescue, and after he removed the blade he taught me the safe way for a kid to shave. That was only ONE blade. Can you imagine if it were six? I could've easily gotten the part of the cop that Mr. Blonde hacked up in *Reservoir Dogs*.

Gillette. Back off! We don't need a razor that can shave a porcupine bare. Nor do we need a kung fu grip handle that vibrates while playing Santana/Rob Thomas songs. And we certainly don't need a bathroom weapon either. Here's what we want: a razor that cuts hair . . . got it?

№017

Robert Ramon
For making wine look cheap.

THE FACTS

When a waiter asks, "Shall I unscrew it for you, sir?", I always feel less than aristocratic.

Perhaps you have heard that cork is becoming extinct? Or that there is a shortage? Or that harvesting it harms the environment? These are all FALSE rumors. Cork comes from a tree—the bark from the cork oak tree, to be exact. This tree is NOT cut down for cork extraction; only the bark is removed. This harvesting occurs about every nine years. A cork tree's life span is about two hundred years.

Cork oak trees provide extensive biodiversity. They protect the soil from drying out, and some wildlife even depends upon the human cultivation of these cork forests for its survival. NOT harvesting cork actually HURTS the environment.

"Cork taint" is the supposed spoiling of wine due to the use of cork. Corking, as it is also called, can be found in about 1 percent to 7 percent of bottles (depending on which study you believe). Curiously, cork taint still occurs even with the use of synthetic stoppers and screw caps. Hmmm . . .

Robert Ramon invented his synthetic pseudo-cork in the eighties. Keep in mind that the "decade of excess" wasn't exactly full of bright beverage ideas (e.g., Crystal Pepsi and New Coke).

[you] RIFE!

Which do you think is healthier for our planet, cork or synthetic? Robert corkscrewed us with this stupid stopper. And if a winery tells you synthetic is superior in any way, it's bullshit; they are just being cheap bastards AND hurting the environment. We all know where you should be sticking that fake cork!

Mary Kay Letourneau
For gettin' it on with a thirteen-year-old.

THE FACTS

In June of 1996, thirteen-year-old Vili Fualaau was taken to the police station with his teacher, Mary Kay Letourneau, after a policeman thought something suspicious was going on with the two of them in Mary's parked minivan. They were let go after the boy's mother vouched for Mary. A few days later, for the first time, the teacher and pupil did the deed. Apparently, Vili won a $20 bet with his classmate for bangin' teach. About eight months later, after having sex three hundred to four hundred times with the boy, Mary was ratted out by her husband's cousin. Consequently, the mother of four was arrested. At that time, she was five months pregnant with Vili's child. Since she was pregnant, the police gave her a reduced suspended sentence of six months in jail. A month after she was released, the statutory rapist got caught with Vili again in a car with the windows fogged up. Mary was sent back to prison with another bun in the oven. This time she spent six and a half years in the slammer. Now she is free and married to her youthful, but legal, beau. The licentious couple will have a great story for their grandkids!

[you] RIFE!

A random mother says lovingly to her child, "Hurry up, Billy, it's your first day of sixth grade, you don't want to be late! Now remember: walk straight to school, don't talk to strangers, just say no to drugs, and don't let the teacher play with Mr. Pee Pee."

Mary, you thought your sexual acts with your child soul mate were "fate," but everyone else called it "rape." There is no sugarcoating it—you're a pedophile. Now parents have to suspect the intentions of female schoolteachers around their children.

Mary Kay, because of you, I hear Wal-Mart now sells chastity belts during the back-to-school rush.

THE FACTS

On the last day of 1997, Michael Kennedy died in a ski accident. Sonny Bono died on the slopes five days later. Both good skiers. Both hit trees. Now both dead. Even if they had been wearing helmets, neither would be alive today. Unfortunately, when famous people die, it attracts the press. Stories like these blow the danger of skiing out of proportion, and now some states are discussing unnecessary mandatory helmet laws. In fact, many resorts already have these rules enforced. Take note: There was no "crime scene investigation" for Michael's or Sonny's death. My malicious jumping tree theory still remains inconclusive.

Believe it or not, deadly skiing accidents are rare, with under forty per year in the U.S. Please note, more than three hundred Americans die each year falling in the bathtub. Currently, there are no available studies analyzing the difficulty of shampooing while wearing head protection.

[you] RIFE!

In case you were born after 1980, Sonny Bono was a singer-songwriter most famous for performing with former wife Cher in their variety show. The high school dropout married four times before becoming the mayor of Palm Springs. He was kind of goofy but, for the most part, he was an okay guy. Unfortunately, he died while skiing without a helmet, so he made the RIFE list.

On the other hand we have Michael Kennedy. Thanks, Mikey. You died hitting a tree while playing ski football. What is ski football, you ask? It's apparently a deadly skiing game you play when you want to avoid statutory rape charges from an alleged affair with the family's underage babysitter.

The more recent tragedy that happened to the Thuringian minister-president and a forty-one-year-old woman only confuse matters more. The helmet-less woman died instantly during a collision with the heavily headed, helmet-wearing prime minister. Now we see that headgear can kill too.

Take note, usually people who die while skiing do it by going way too fast and hitting a tree. Here is an idea: If you want to avoid death, don't do that! Slow the fuck down, and if you see a trunk—turn.

№02000

McGraw-Hill
For promoting the Y2K fear.

THE FACTS

Y2K stands for: [Y]ou've got [2] be [K]idding!

In 1996, McGraw-Hill Publishers changed the name of a 1984 nonfiction book and rereleased it as *The Year 2000 Computing Crisis*. The book took as its focus the number of software programs that stored years as two digits instead of four—for example, 99 instead of 1999—and discussed the potentially devastating effects this would have on our computer-run world when the clocks rolled over at midnight at the turn of the millennium and long-working computer systems broke down. As most of you well know, it was blown more than slightly out of proportion. So if you are still in your bomb shelter, you can come out now. It was all a hoax.

[you] RIFE!

If FDR were alive in the late nineties, he would have revised his statement to say, "We have nothing to fear but Y2K itself!" The whole world thought we would be swallowed by a black hole and transported to some Amish farm in Ohio when the ball dropped for the new millennium. Many stocked up on food, water, and guns waiting for the apocalyptic computer meltdown. If you weren't at least a little scared, you were lying. Some even withdrew their life savings from their banks and hid it under their ammunition crates (little did they know they were eight years too early).

The showdown between the modern world and a couple of forgotten computer code digits was quite anticlimactic. The only winners in the cyber-war were a couple of overstocked army surplus stores, a bunch of pocket-protector-wearing techies, and, of course, McGraw-Hill. About the only thing that happed was that London's Millennium Wheel failed to operate (but for unrelated reasons). Thanks for the good times!

№021 | Alcohol
For being the devil's nectar.

THE FACTS

Alcoholism was declared an illness by the American Medical Association in 1956. E.M. Jellinek wrote a book called *The Disease Concept of Alcoholism* in 1960, further exploring the topic. Even the National Council on Alcoholism and Drug Dependence believes alcoholism is a mental addiction that drives someone to drink. Alcohol has such a stronghold on humans that the U.S. government even tried to outlaw liquor during Prohibition, but it just didn't stick. The sauce kept calling us back!

[you] RIFE!

If a drunk were to explain the effects of alcohol, he'd tell you what's what (probably while slurring and uncontrollably spitting in your face). Alcohol could force you to lose your job, your girlfriend, and your license. It may enable sexual relations with unsightly riffraff. It can give you headaches and mood swings, and it can make you puke or black out, and even poison you. It can take control of your motor skills, forcing you to stick your hand where it doesn't belong. It makes you say things you'll regret and causes bad breath. It also inhibits your ability to operate heavy machinery. I even had a buddy in college who was forced by alcohol to pee his pants in his sleep . . . (Okay, it was me. I did it. And that poor futon was never quite the same.)

Some people have the audacity to disagree with the claims that alcoholism is a disease and an addiction. Obviously, they were never left alone in a college dorm room with a full bottle of cinnamon schnapps when they were sixteen years old. Hell, you might even believe that alcohol was an airborne disease if you saw the way that firewater jumped from the bottle to my throat.

Well anyway, if you ever find yourself lying on a park bench covered with newspapers and reeking of your own vomit after being kicked out of the house, you can blame alcoholism for being a disease. But mostly, you can blame doctors for NEVER finding a cure. Cheers!

N°022

The inventor of plastic packaging
For causing unnecessary ER visits.

THE FACTS

Okay, after extensive and exhaustive research (twenty minutes of searching on Google), the inventor of plastic packaging could not be uncovered. Apparently the creator is so ashamed of his creation, he has gone to great lengths to conceal his identity. Well, whoever you are, we still loathe you.

The fact is, plastic packaging sucks. I am referring to the vacuum-sealed clamshell kind. You know the type, the one that appears to be superglued around all the edges, making it nearly impossible to extract what's inside.

This near-lethal packaging puts about six thousand Americans in the emergency room every year with sliced arteries and dangling fingers in critical need of stitches. With seasonal gift giving, a noticeable spike in emergency room visits occurs around Christmastime.

[you] RIFE!

Prior to opening these packages, you should consider calling the fire department for assistance, because you need nothing less than the Jaws of Life to break into the casing. If you do it yourself, you may still be speed-dialing emergency services after you sever your finger with a utility knife.

Apparently this type of packaging reduces theft. Whoop-de-fuckin'-doo! Get some magnetic buzzers like everyone else. It is dangerous, consumers hate it, and the additional plastic is certainly not helping our environment.

And if anyone finds out who invented this shit, let me know.

№ 023

O.J. Simpson's (first) jury
For letting a guilty man walk free.

THE FACTS

On July 22, 1994, O.J. Simpson answered the question "How do you plead?" at his arraignment with "Absolutely 100 percent not guilty, your honor." The prosecution thought it had substantial evidence to convict the ex–football hero. But after months of drama, the trial ended. Half of all Americans watched live to hear the verdict agree with Simpson's original not-guilty plea. The rest of the world was dumbfounded.

Over a year later, a civil trial jury unanimously found O.J. liable for the wrongful deaths of Goldman and Brown. He was ordered to pay $33 million in damages.

It is estimated that you have better than a two-to-one chance of getting away with murder. So if you are looking for a little extra shove to snuff out that irksome spouse, and you have the bankroll for first-rate counsel, the odds are scarily favorable for you to get away with murder. Just make sure you do it in America, where your chance is about 58 percent. Your odds to dodge a conviction in other countries are less favorable: Britain, 26 percent; Russia, 10 percent; China, 2 percent; and Japan, 0.03 percent.

[you] RIFE!

Where did they find this jury anyway? Pardons "R" Us? After the verdict was read, I was waiting for the *Candid Camera* crew to reveal themselves. But they never did. What seemed an impossible Hail Mary pass ended in a shocking home-team defeat. Perhaps the jury was hypnotically dazzled by the overly catchy lawyer's rhyme: "If it doesn't fit, you must acquit."

And, of course, we have the lawyers to point fingers at. What can I say? (No—really—what can I say without being sued?) Anyway, we learned that with a flawed system and lots of cash, the power of self-preservation should never be underestimated. So remember the odds if you have a taste for blood. I guess the question is, "Do you feel lucky?" Well, do ya, punk?

Luckily, karma came around to right the wrong with O.J.'s Vegas robbery verdict.

№024

Guy standing up at a concert
For ruining a good time.

THE FACTS

Live music is one of my personal passions. The anticipation of lights dimming and that initial uproar of the crowd cheering in unison are unparalleled. The first riff gives me goose bumps. The experience can be exhilarating for many. Unfortunately, it's usually ruined by some annoying jerkwad.

[you] RIFE!

The guy who just won't sit down in his seat ruins the concert experience. Let's get one thing straight: Concerts only have two options in regards to seating. One is an actual seat. The other is no seat at all; it's just general admission, standing room only. In the case of the latter, it's okay to stand, jump up and down, bump into people, rush the stage, and even crowd-surf. However, if you paid for a seat, USE IT. Stand up for the first couple songs, showing your support while waving your arms, and then sit the fuck down. You are being irritating and you're pissing off everyone behind you. This type of behavior is unacceptable and will no longer be tolerated.

Other guys (and girls) that make the concertgoing experience less than enjoyable:

- Guy too drunk and belligerent at a concert. (Just pass out already.)
- Guy throwing bottles at a concert. (Great idea, dipshit.)
- Guy singing too loudly at a concert. (Sing, just not louder than the band.)
- Girl screeching when her favorite song starts at a concert. (Please stop.)
- Guy wearing a T-shirt of the band he is seeing at a concert. (Don't be that guy.)

№025 | Richard Gere
For making it a sin to own a gerbil.

THE FACTS

America. The land of gossip, rumors, and dirty laundry. Our constant craving for celebrity mischief is overwhelming. Especially if it's of a sexual nature. The paparazzi continually serve it up fresh, and we keep gorging.

As rumors go, this is a doozy . . . The allegation goes that Richard Gere supposedly went to the emergency room with a foreign object lodged up his rectum in 1993. An X-ray was taken and the object in question was revealed to be a gerbil. He was then rushed into surgery, where the top surgeons in Los Angeles extracted the asphyxiated rodent.

Okay, I admit it, we had a few gerbils and hamsters when we were children. However, thanks to Richard, it is very embarrassing to admit. So yeah, I may have spun poor Peattie on the ottoman until he was dizzy—but I NEVER partook in rodent ramming.

[you] RIFE!

So who is really to blame for this nonsense? Some say Gere's nemesis Sylvester Stallone. Apparently, they rubbed each other the wrong way during a lunch break while on the set of some crappy movie. They were in a car and Gere was responsible for some greasy mustard dribbling on Sly's thigh. It's unclear if the grease penetrated Stallone's pants, but there must have been some dry cleaning involved. It came to be a fight, with the officer and (so-called) gentleman getting Stallone kicked off the movie's set.

Quite frankly, Mr. Gere only made matters worse: He never denied the gerbil claim when it was alleged. But mostly, it was the public's fault for wanting to believe such an intrusive rumor. Either way, if you own a gerbil, make sure you "hide" it before your friends arrive, NOT while they're there.

Nº026 | Coppertone
For inventing sunless tanning lotion.

THE FACTS

Soaking up the sun used to be great. You got a nice golden-brown skin tone and acquired more than a daily dose of vitamin D. Unfortunately, after many years of studies, we found out that excessive sun exposure is linked to skin cancer. So what do we do to compensate? We use sunblock to enjoy a carefree time under the sun. Unfortunately, instances of skin cancer are not declining. Recent studies are suggesting agents in sun protection lotion may be causing cancer as well. I know, I know—damned if you do, and damned if you don't.

The Skin Cancer Foundation estimates that more than six hundred thousand new cases of skin cancer arise each year. Is there a way to avoid the sun and still be tan? One solution is to apply brown shoe polish liberally. The other is sunless tanning cream. However, beware of misuse, as you may be forced to join the comedy circuit with Carrot Top.

[you] RIFE!

Coppertone invented sunless tanning lotion. The company's scientists must have secretly added a chemical to its sunless ointment that causes color-blindness (similar to beer goggles). This must be why people think they look good after using it. TAKE OFF your shady spectacles. It's not a Caribbean tan, you're ORANGE! In case you were wondering, humans are NOT inherently pumpkin-colored. But if you still wish for a sunless tanned physique, and you aren't expecting an Oscar win (yeah, we are talkin' about you, Charlize), you can always give it a try.

Be realistic when it comes to skin cancer protection. Pretending you are a vampire is not the solution. Turning yourself into bunny food isn't recommended either. Go play in the sun with some applied SPF and try to avoid using Crisco as a tanning accelerant. Just don't go to extremes. Here's a helpful mental chart to follow: If the sun gives you blisters, or if self-bronzer turns you into a Cheeto, then you've gone overboard. Use common sense: Too much of anything is bad.

№ 027

THE FACTS

Usually, everyone's life trots along at a steady pace. There may be slight ups and subtle downs that you have control over. And we have to admit, in the heat of the moment, most seemingly significant choices are actually minuscule in the grand scheme of things. Typically, what defines our integrity and character is just a handful of split second decisions. These decisions can make or break us, and sometimes . . . it can affect the masses. And yet the right choice always seemed so clearly *black and white* in hindsight. Or, in BP's eyes, just black. Black for the oil they leaked, black in their neglect, and black for the human and environmental casualties they caused.

[you] RIFE!

I could talk all day about blowout preventers, bad legislation, Minerals Management Service, greedy oil supermajors, Transocean, Halliburton, and a slimy yacht racing CEO. But I am not going to bore you with the details—you already know it's a catastrophic headache that even a tanker-sized Tylenol can't cure. So let's focus on the root of the crude mess in America's gulf. Whose decision was it? When was the moment? And what the fuck? Well, it was BP—it was clearly when they gave priority to profits in lieu of safety—and obviously, it's because they are affiliated with Satan.

As it turns out, this is another one of those, "How did we not see this thing coming?" moments. Not only is BP really terrific at filling up the gulf with hazardous sludge, but they are also really crafty at breaking safety records and paying fines to avoid criminal prosecution. During the past few years, OSHA slapped BP with 760, of what they call, "egregious and willful" safety violations. Whereas Sunoco, Conoco-Phillips, Citgo, and Exxon only had 19 combined. And remember, these oil giants weren't exactly at the top of Mother Theresa's holiday mailing list either.

So if you see something dark brown floating in the water, I'll bet you some black gold that you're either in a Bill Murray movie or you're sitting on a beach in the Gulf of Mexico. Be sure to thank BP for skimping on the ounce of prevention that could have been worth barrels of cure.

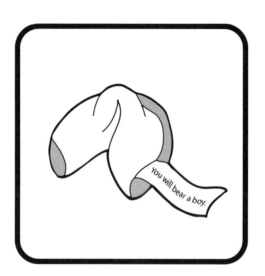

№028

Chinese boys
For being so valuable.

THE FACTS

In China, girls rule and boys duel. Here's the problem: In 1979, Chinese ruler Deng Xiaoping introduced the one-child policy because his country's population was growing out of control. The law stayed in effect for thirty years. Essentially, the Chinese government would punish couples with ridiculous fines for having more than one child. It even forced sterilization or IUD insertion after a mother had her first child. What was the fallout? For every one hundred girls born, there were one hundred and twenty boys born. The problem was that most Chinese couples preferred boys and went to great lengths to have one.

So why are there so many extra Y chromosomes in the communist nation? Don't ask, 'cause you really don't want to know. But I can tell you that now ultrasounds are illegal in China. You can still get one in some cases, but the doctors won't tell you the baby's sex. Also, two doctors must be present during the procedure, and everyone is watched on closed-circuit TV. Say cheese!

[you] RIFE!

So what makes boys so valuable in China? Isn't the song called "Thank Heaven for Little Girls"? You see, birthing a son allows a couple to carry the family legacy. But even more, bearing a boy is the parents' retirement plan. It's expected that male children will support their parents in old age. That makes sense . . . nobody wants to end up in a rest home (see RIFE №080).

What does all of this mean? Well, right now there are thirty-two million more boys than girls under the age of twenty in China. And those boys will need brides (or at least some action). But they aren't going to be finding it . . . Enter the crime scene. Some Chinese parents and criminals go to unthinkable lengths to profit from this bad situation. Boys are kidnapped and sold to sonless parents. Girls are sold overseas or kidnapped, raised, and forced into marriage. And soon there will be an excessive imbalance of elderly people needing support. And all these poor boys will be competing over a few higher-paying jobs and even fewer women. I hope China has a plan for this mess. If not, the government better start drafting for Catholic priesthood and give serious tax rebates for gay marriages.

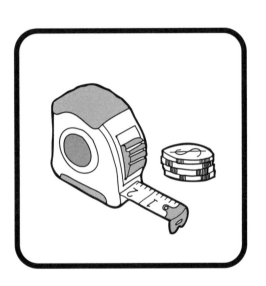

№029

Dick Fuld
For being a greedy CEO.

THE FACTS

If the three magic words in real estate are "location," "location," and "location," then the magic words in corporate America must be "greed," "greed," and "greed."

Lehman Brothers Holdings Inc. was a worldwide financial services firm founded in 1850. If it involved money, banking, or lending, Lehman was doing it—and doing it with a vengeance. The financial company had been on the express train until its startling demise in 2008, when it fell limp.

Dick Fuld was the last chairman and CEO of Lehman Brothers. This pud rammed a hundred-and-fifty-year-old company into the ground because of his gluttonous greed. During his fourteen years of leading Lehman to bankruptcy, his total compensation was around $500 million.

[you] RIFE!

Dick, you certainly live up to your name. You really ruined it for everyone. You got fat stacks while at the same time dicking over your company—not to mention giving the shaft to America's economy. This peckerhead promoted subprime mortgages to unqualified borrowers, and then spooged out even more money by turning the risky debt into bonds. These sketchy debts went sour and brought the world to its knee pads. Pricks like Dick have led the world to financial disaster, and they're the reason the U.S. dollar isn't worth a single square of toilet paper.

Mr. Fuld fooled us all. I guess he forgot that it was America's economy he was playing with, not a game of pocket pool. So keep your eye out for cheats like him. Remember, if it seems too good to be true, then it probably is. And if you are a conglomerate, make sure you pay your CEOs appropriately, judging their success on length, not girth.

№030

THE FACTS

I want my pizza hot and delivered to my stoop in under thirty minutes or I ain't paying for it, DAMMIT! When we were kids, we used to wait by the door with a stopwatch! Those were the days of pizza hot and fast. Too bad—that era is long gone.

Domino's Pizza was founded in 1960, and it began the "30 Minutes or It's Free" campaign in 1973. Thomas Monaghan, the founder of Domino's Pizza, decided to pull the twenty-year-long campaign in 1993. At that time, a couple of lawsuits were decided against his company because the guarantee promoted reckless employee driving. One accident, resulting in death, fetched $2.8 million, while another driver, whose head and back were injured, was awarded $78 million.

[you] RIFE!

Thomas shouldn't have caved in so easily. And he should have hired better lawyers. Don't get me wrong, I usually root for the little guy, but hell, so many large companies become such magnets for huge lawsuits that you can't help but feel a little remorse for them. Regardless, he's the reason you can't get fast pizza anymore.

It sucks when your stomach is growling and you know the pizza is going to be late, and most likely cold. Nonetheless, try to give Domino's a break. I know it's hard, but try not to take it out on the delivery guys, as they are only human. Besides, you'd lose your appetite anyway if a family of four's blood ended up splattered on your pizza box.

And if you STILL want pizza in under thirty minutes, move to India, Israel, or Mexico, because Domino's still has the guarantee there!

№031 | Guabntánamo Bay
For producing terrorists.

THE FACTS

If we only knew the real facts . . . This account is more of a guesstimate.

[you] RIFE!

The Guantánamo Bay detention facility consists of several prison camps operated by the United States in Cuba. It has been in operation since 1987 and is scheduled to close down during the Obama administration. The lockup has been under scrutiny for torturous interrogation techniques since the Bush administration.

Imagine for a minute that you are captured by another government's military. You are treated worse than a Michael Vick voodoo doll in the hands of PETA. You're then flown halfway around the world to a place you've never heard of. There you are locked up, interrogated, and tortured for something you may or may not have done. You are held without charges and without a trial. All around you see countless victims being violated and grotesquely treated. This goes on for six years before you are released. What would you do about it? Seek revenge?

I'm sure you can find some studies to support claims that prison camp detainment and torture builds excellent leadership qualities. Thanks, America—you are creating super-terrorists!

Rumsfeld, Cheney, and Bush promoted torture and violence in the wake of 9/11. This "us or them" attitude was wrong. Especially when we didn't know who "they" were! It's just adding fuel to the fire!

Then again, it takes one kind of person to suggest torture, and a totally different type to implement it. The U.S. soldiers who carried out these inhumane orders should be ashamed. Who did you think you were? Jack Nicholson? Trust me—we can handle the truth. Were you so brainwashed that you couldn't see right from wrong? I admire and appreciate that you protect our country, but try to be a human being too.

Here's the problem: If the prisoners were not terrorists prior to being detained, you can bet your waterboard they will be once they're freed. Job well done!

NºO32

Tweekers
For putting Sudafed behind the counter.

THE FACTS

A tweeker is someone who uses methamphetamines, a.k.a. crystal meth. It is one dirty drug. It's usually smoked, but can be injected, snorted, or even shoved up the ass (with or without Richard's gerbil). After the drug is taken, meth enters the bloodstream and stimulates the dopamine receptors. This makes the user enter a state of euphoria for up to twelve hours. The "high" is similar to cocaine but lasts much longer.

Sudafed, and other brands of decongestants, contain one of the ingredients used in the manufacture of crystal meth. The pseudoephedrine is cooked out of these medicines and is then combined with other agents to make the drug. This means people who make crystal meth need to get their hands on as much Sudafed as possible. And therein lays the problem.

[you] RIFE!

So your nose is stuffed up? Well then, when you get to the drugstore, head toward the pharmacy counter, because you will not find any useful medicine on the shelves. And don't forget your ID, because you will get carded. And I hope it's not a lingering cold, because you are only allowed nine grams per month. Law enforcement has also added MethCheck software to most pharmacies. So if everyone in your family gets a cold or your allergies flare up, you may just be investigated for cooking meth.

Thanks a lot, tweekers! Luckily, your punishment fits your nasty lifestyle. Your body will get sores all over and your teeth will crack and rot out, and you'll have the sensation of bugs crawling all over you skin. Are you feeling itchy?

№033

Chaka
For graffiti-covered cities.

THE FACTS

Chaka, a.k.a. Daniel Ramos, was an infamous graffiti tagger in the early nineties. He got his name from a furry little character found on the TV show *Land of the Lost*. Every night, from 11 PM to 5 AM, Ramos would arm himself with about eight stolen cans of black and silver spray paint. He tagged signs and buildings throughout the West Coast with CHAKA. It was estimated by authorities that the tagger painted his name on ten thousand surfaces, resulting in more than $500,000 in property damage (although he later claimed the number to be closer to forty thousand tags).

After the conviction, he was sentenced to three years probation and fifteen hundred hours of community service (graffiti cleanup). Later, he was busted for trespassing on an L.A. city golf course and for possession of marijuana. He had another brush with the law in 1998, when he got caught stealing shoes at a department store. He was sentenced to jail for fifteen months. The tagger even had the audacity to scratch his name inside the elevator of the courthouse he was tried in.

[you] RIFE!

Brilliant, Ramos. Because of you and taggers like you, spray paint is now under lock and key. You cluttered cities with senseless graffiti and you stole thousands of cans of spray paint. Now, to this day, we have to track down a sales clerk just to buy some damn paint.

Unfortunately, Ramos gave a great art form a bad name.

Luckily, Chaka has been out of the limelight for a while. However, he resurfaced to do an art show in Los Angeles in April 2009. I just hope he keeps his paint on the canvas this time. And by the way, I hope Chaka doesn't leave his art unattended in the wee hours of the night . . .

№034

Mark David Chapman
For robbing us of John Lennon.

THE FACTS

On December 8, 1980, Mark David Chapman shot John Lennon three times in the back and once in the shoulder. This bloody display happened outside of Lennon's New York apartment late in the evening. One of the bullets pierced Lennon's aorta, resulting in severe blood loss. Police officers rushed him to the hospital in their cruiser. Unfortunately, he was pronounced dead on arrival.

After Chapman shot Lennon, he stayed at the scene, pulled out his copy of *The Catcher in the Rye*, and waited for the police to arrive. He was willingly apprehended. Later, at the station, he actually told the police, "I'm sure the large part of me is Holden Caulfield, who is the main person in the book, the small part of me must be the devil." (Yeah, I don't know what that means either . . . I think the book's a good read, but it doesn't cause demonic possession!)

Chapman was sentenced to twenty years to life. He has been denied parole five times.

[you] RIFE!

Mark Chapman shocked the world with his ungodly actions. Not only did he destroy a rock legend, he also assassinated an icon for peace. John Lennon used his fame wisely to promote social change and hope. His antiwar message prompted the era's younger generation to be active and aware of the world around them. John Lennon's ideals will live on in his music, even if we're forced to soldier on without him.

In 2008, Chapman gave an interview and admitted he was sorry for shooting Lennon. He said he was feeling like a "nobody" and just wanted to be something other than that. Well, congratulations, you got your wish. The next time you need attention, try setting yourself on fire.

 | **Katherine Harris**
For giving us our dumbest president.

THE FACTS

Katherine Harris was Florida's secretary of state and a key figure in the controversial 2000 U.S. presidential election between Al Gore and George W. Bush. It was initially thought that Bush won by a large margin. However, much to the dismay of Fox News, the actual results ended up much closer. Bush had only won by a handful of votes and this triggered recount hysteria.

Everyone waited anxiously to see who would be awarded the presidency. During the process, we found out that Harris had many ballots tossed out due to voter error and inferior counting machinery. She also unjustly denied voter registration to thousands prior to the election (most of whom were Democrats). In an effort to disrupt the recount, Katherine halted attempts at hand recounts, which led to her being challenged in court. At first she was victorious, but then the Florida Supreme Court overturned the ruling. After that, the U.S. Supreme Court stuck its judicial nose into the fiasco and stopped the recount again. It ruled in favor of Gore for a continued recount but, ironically, decided that time had run out and declared Bush the victor.

The whole event was a debacle. Essentially, the frequent starting and stopping of the recount process did not allow adequate time to finish the task. After five weeks of edge-of-your-seat drama, we had a schmuck president-elect named George. (Despite losing the electoral college vote, Al Gore still won the popular vote.)

[you] RIFE!

Katherine, you signed an oath to uphold the Constitution, but apparently autographed it with only twelve-hour lipstick. You screwed us. George W. Bush would've never been elected president if the recount had been fair. So it's your fault we went to war with Iraq, had all of our phones illegally tapped, federal prosecutors were unjustly fired, oil prices quadrupled, and the whole world ended up in a recession. Not to mention we would've probably found a cure for cancer by allowing stem cell research and bin Laden would more than likely be a greasy spot on some missile head by now. Hope your loyalty was worth it. Shame on you! There's an old saying in Florida that goes, "Fool voters once, shame on . . . shame on you. Fool voters . . . you can't get fooled again, Florida."

№ 36-24-36

Ruth Handler
For making girls bitter.

THE FACTS

The Barbie doll was invented in 1959 by Ruth Handler. Ruth was a cofounder of Mattel and named the doll after her own daughter. She noticed that most dolls were infants and felt that it was time for a change. The invention was simple: a grown-up doll for children to play with. Barbie was an instant success.

Barbie's supposed to be a "real" woman, but, besides having no nipples, her measurements originally were 39-18-33 (bow-chicka-wow-wow). This sparked much controversy with critics, their argument being that Barbie was modeled after an "adult" toy, and the measurements were based on male fantasy. Barbie's bust and hips were later adjusted due to criticism. However, the proportions are still impractical and will set you back about thirty-five grand in plastic surgery.

[you] RIFE!

Mrs. Handler is responsible for crushing prepubescent aspirations. Barbie's measurements create unrealistic expectations for young girls to live up to. Ruth claimed that Barbie's busty bosom would build up a girl's self-assurance. However, since it is physically impossible to have these measurements, it actually has a negative effect on a girl's self-esteem. Don't worry, boys: I hear there are talks of reducing Ken's bulge size as well.

Come on, Ruth! The world is superficial enough. We don't need to encourage little Jane's bulimia and boob job, nor to promote young Billy's steroid use and penis pump.

Ruth Handler was not all bad. Ironically, after she had breast cancer and a mastectomy, she invented a prosthetic breast called the Nearly Me. Many breast cancer victims found relief in the prosthesis, as it matched the weight and density of a natural breast. Karma's a bitch, but we forgive you.

№ 037 | Tiger
For actually being a cheetah!

THE FACTS

Prior to November 2009, if Tiger Woods stood on a roof and shouted down to fans, "I am a golden god," nobody would have disputed it—not even Tiger. And why not? Woods has won fourteen major golf championships, is the youngest to achieve the career grand slam, and has held the No. 1 position longer than any other golfer. Oh, and he made more money than any other athlete in 2008—$110 million.

Believe it or not, Mr. Woods originally made it into this book "for not letting anyone else win"! It was a lighthearted story that crowned my (ex-)sports hero king of golf and applauded him for being an all-around swell guy. But NO—what we get instead is a strange car accident involving a tree, a fire hydrant, and a nine iron. And then WHOA Nelly—and Rachel . . . and Kalika . . . and Mindy . . . and Jamie . . . and another one named Jamiee . . . and Cori . . . and Holly . . . and Joslyn . . .

Who knows if they are all legit? And really, who cares about the number after the tally gets higher than you can count on a single golf glove?

[you] RIFE!

That was the last straw for me. I no longer watch pro sports. I've switched to less scandalous professional entertainment—late night Cinemax.

Tiger made us realize that cute fuzzy gophers weren't the only sneaky rodents roaming the golf course. But if you're still a Tiger fan, don't worry: If he's anything like his furry friends, he'll burrow his way out of his hole in no time singing the *Caddyshack* theme song. In fact, I'm sure by the time you are reading this, Tiger will be back at the top of his game and the forgetful public will be cheering for the cheater and buying sports drinks with his ten-timing face printed on the label.

NºO38

Peter Cooper Hewitt
For giving us horrible lighting.

THE FACTS

American Peter Cooper Hewitt patented the first mercury vapor lamp in 1901. This low-pressure lamp was the very first prototype of today's modern fluorescent lights. Thanks for nothing!

[you] RIFE!

I wish fluorescent lights would go away. I support great light quality and horrible efficiency! GO INCANDESCENT!

Yeah, yeah, yeah . . . fluorescents are better for the environment. Unfortunately, they give off horrible light quality, and they flicker and buzz. The fluorescent light is like the Prius of cars. It's really economical and a good idea, but it's ugly and we can't stop it!

Apparently, Ned Flanders is the only one who likes them. He once said, "Oooh, they hum like angels! You're never lonely if you've got a fluorescent light!"

When someone gets a great idea, a lightbulb pops up above his head, but NOT a fluorescent tube! There is good reason for this: It's because, besides taking a few seconds to flicker on, the fluorescent tube was a crappy idea with poor execution. And thanks to Hewitt's technology, we now have terrible lighting in countless offices, hospitals, and municipal buildings around the world.

Fluorescent lights downgrade the quality of any space. And their melancholic glow is enough to drive anyone off the edge. How many people have slipped into chronic depression because of badly lit offices? Well, I don't know the answer to that, but even one is too many (unless, of course, it's that one asshole who never refills the printer paper).

№039

Dr. Martin Cooper
For making us too available!

THE FACTS

Dr. Martin Cooper invented the cellular phone. He came up with the sophisticated technology responsible for the cell phone when he was the director of research and development at Motorola. Now he's the CEO of the ArrayComm antenna corporation.

[you] RIFE!

Thanks a lot, doc; now we are available, all the time.

The mobile phone could be claimed as one of the greatest inventions of the twentieth century. However, I would argue against it. Really, all it does is make us reachable every second of every day. Is that a good thing? Is the trade-off worth it? Do you want to "get away"? Well, too bad, you can't 'cause you own a cell phone. And of course, you can never NOT answer your cell phone because then you're an asshole phone-dodger. Not to mention that you always get that itch of curiosity to find out what the call is about.

Besides making us constantly available, the mobile device is probably causing us to develop cancer, making us infertile and impotent due to the digital radiation, and creating a whole new array of repetitive motion injuries. I know Travolta became smart with one in *Phenomenon*, but I would prefer to avoid a brain tumor! And quite frankly, I am getting tired of loud phone conversations everywhere I go. It happens waiting in line, on airplanes, at restaurants, in elevators and movie theaters—enough already. Stop the insanity! If you are going to do it, learn how to use your "inside" voice. I guess one benefit of cell phone overexposure is knowing that the loud-talking dickwad in line at Starbucks gabbing on his phone is going to eventually have his penis fall off from harmful mobile phone emissions! So at least we have that to look forward to!

№040

Edward A. Murphy
For creating a "law" for stuff to go wrong.

THE FACTS

Definition: Murphy's Law—if anything can go wrong, it will.

The suggestive saying was named after Capt. Edward A. Murphy, an engineer working on an Air Force project at Edwards Air Force Base. A rocket deceleration test failed to record needed data. Murphy discovered the failure was the result of his assistant wiring a transducer backwards. Murphy got a little pissed about the mistake and said, "If there is any way to do it wrong, he'll find it." The project manager wrote this down on his list of "laws" and called it Murphy's Law.

Shortly afterward, Dr. John Paul Stapp, one of the test riders for the deceleration track, was in an important press conference. He was asked a question regarding safety and how the test riders avoided being hurt during the rocket-sled tests. He said that their good safety record was due to a firm belief in Murphy's Law and the challenge to try and evade it. The saying stuck after being published in a few journals.

[you] RIFE!

Thanks a lot, Murph! You gave it a name . . .

Now anything that can go wrong will, at the worst possible time, and in the worst possible way. All because of your little hissy fit!

Here are a few other unnecessary sayings that precipitate bad things happening just because they were given a name: crying wolf, the domino effect, alcoholism, schadenfreude, and the Bermuda triangle. Even when someone says, "Don't drop that!", you are certainly ten times more likely to. When analyzed, it's more of a chicken-and-egg debate—if there were no chicken there would be no egg—hence no debate. What we have learned is that when you drop a piece of toast with peanut butter on the floor, you can be sure it will land on the bad side. But let's say it actually landed gooey side up (and you took the three-second rule into account). Would you still eat it anyway?

№041 | Clarence Thomas
For calling it "Long Dong Silver."

THE FACTS

Sexual harassment laws are relatively new to society. The United States adopted the 1964 Civil Rights Act, but even then, the first lawsuits filed under its auspices did not happen until the 1970s. Since then, interpretation of the law has broadened.

Unfortunately for Supreme Court Justice Clarence Thomas, he was not immune to these laws during his Supreme Court nomination proceedings in 1981. The sexual harassment allegations from Anita Hill ignited a media frenzy prior to Thomas's appointment. The nationally televised hearing sparked many longstanding water-cooler jokes over such phrases as "There is a pubic hair in my Coke!" and a certain penis in question named "Long Dong Silver." In the end, the hearing failed to substantiate Anita's claims. These events didn't help Clarence's already skimpy qualifications. Nonetheless, this man made it to the highest judicial position in the land. The Senate elected him with a 52-48 vote (which was the smallest margin in Supreme Court history).

[you] RIFE!

Sexual harassment trials in later years that sided against men show us Clarence acted similarly to guilty parties. Also, Clarence said Anita was a "mediocre" employee. If this were true, why did Mr. Thomas hire her twice? It has to be one or the other: She was either a good employee, or he just wanted to sleep with her. Something smells fishy!

Did he rape her? No, but he still made crude sexual remarks to Anita and made her feel uncomfortable in the workplace. This type of accusation should not be associated with a Supreme Court justice.

So the next time you are thinking about discussing your pubes at the water cooler with a member of the opposite sex, remember that there is a good chance you can get away with it. Hell, you may even be promoted (especially if you are a Republican).

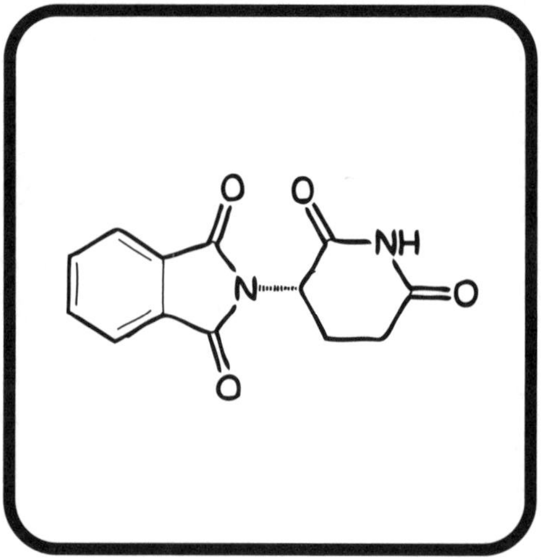

Nº042

Chemie Grünenthal
For causing thalidomide birth defects.

THE FACTS

Wilhelm Kunz, a trained pharmacist, discovered thalidomide by accident while synthesizing drug compounds for the German pharmaceutical company Chemie Grünenthal. The drug was used to treat morning sickness in pregnant women. And while it was quite effective at treating nausea, it was also tragically efficient at disrupting the normal development of fetuses. Thousands of children in countries around the world were born with birth defects that included malformed limbs and supernumerary appendages.

[you] RIFE!

Herr Kuntz, *Sie haben es für alle ruiniert!* What were you thinking? You were a pharmacist, not a scientist. You were trained to distribute drugs, not make them. And shame on you, Chemie Grünenthal! Your greed kept you from properly testing thalidomide before releasing it to the public. You were blinded by visions of beaucoup Deutschemarks in your eyes and sold it anyway. More than ten thousand children in forty-six countries were born with deformities because of your neglect. Let's not forget, this is the same kind of bullshit that made Harrison Ford a *Fugitive*.

Nº043

THE FACTS

George W. Bush set us back decades in so many ways. I don't have the time, or energy, to express all of my negative views toward his idiocy. The entire book could be dedicated to his blight. Nonetheless, I will focus on merely a tiny blunder of his reign: "freedom fries."

Bush and his posse decided to rename french fries "freedom fries" after the French opposed the U.S.-led invasion of Iraq. Some conservatives, for a while, boycotted French goods in retaliation as well. Bush's cronies, Robert Ney and Walter Jones, instigated the change in the House of Representatives' cafeterias, which later caught on to various restaurants across the country. They intended it to express our displeasure with France. However, the name change was a ridiculous and childish way to express irritation. Not to mention that french fries come from Belgium. Many argue that there should have been a more intelligent way to show displeasure.

[you] RIFE!

You dickhead! You ruined our world standing. I have tried to mentally block out all of your wrongdoings about as effectively as sunlight through a window. All I can say is: *freedom fries?* Are you serious? This was your quiet temper tantrum against the French for not supporting a meaningless war? That's why French people now call American cheese "idiot cheese."

I leave you with a few of my favorite Bush quotes:

- "See, free nations are peaceful nations. Free nations don't attack each other. Free nations don't develop weapons of mass destruction." October 3, 2003.
- "You teach a child to read, and he or her will be able to pass a literacy test." February 21, 2001.
- "The most important thing is for us to find Osama bin Laden. It is our No. 1 priority and we will not rest until we find him." September 13, 2001.
- "I don't know where bin Laden is. I have no idea and really don't care. It's not that important. It's not our priority." March 13, 2002.

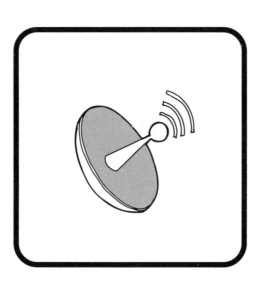

Nº044

Barack Obama
For promoting a dying technology.

THE FACTS

Barack is doing a pretty good job mopping up the Bush mess and presidentially sweeping it under the oval rug. Let's just say he hasn't ruined anything major—*yet*. And I hope by the time you're reading this he hasn't been caught next to an intern with his pants down while signing a communistic health care-reform document.

If you are not aware, Obama has allocated a large wad of cash into America's broadband infrastructure. About $8 billion is being poured into the construction of new broadband Internet networking in hopes of improving connectivity in rural areas.

The allocation of monies is a bit vague. However, I guarantee the cable and phone companies' mouths are salivating to add more customers through cable and improved fiber optic telephone lines. The problem is that this technology is on its way out. The world is going wireless. We should be allocating most of the money to wireless connectivity. If we don't, we are just going to be left with a lot of useless wires blocking our view of the deer and the antelope at play, purple mountain majesties above the fruited plains, and the rockets' red glare!

[you] RIFE!

We know what you are trying to do, Barack—you are trying to create jobs, stimulate the economy, and better America's Internet connectivity at the same time. You even mention how well it worked with our road system back in the day. But why spend time and money laying down thousands of miles of broadband Internet lines in rural areas when it's not economical? Instead, we should be investing in 4G and other wireless technology. Yes, we would still be No. 20 in the world for landlines, but we would be No. 1 in wireless connectivity. Boo-ya! Take that, Japan!

Yes, the idea worked in the past with creating roadways and bridges to improve our economy. However, it's a different era, and we need to allocate our resources intelligently. If you want to invest in old technology, develop better pothole fillers that can last longer than one winter!

Barack, try not to make it on the list again, and stop apologizing for every little thing (it makes you look wimpy).

№045

Albert and Joe Cobble
For making carpet affordable.

THE FACTS

Carpet sucks.

In 1949, the Cobble brothers teamed up with a bedspread company and made the first tufting machinery wide enough to produce carpeting in a single pass. This, along with the use of cheaper backing materials, made wall-to-wall carpet accessible and affordable to the masses. Eventually, carpet became a cheap way to cover unfinished wood floors. This, of course, led the way for scuzzy landlords to quickly resurface floors by covering up stains and chalk outlines in trashy low-rent apartments.

[you] RIFE!

Al and Joe, I blame you for making our living spaces harbor microscopic filthiness. To put it mildly, carpet is disgusting. It looks cheap and trashy. The only way to really clean it is to burn it. Aside from being aesthetically grotesque, it can contain lead, dust mites, allergens, bacteria, and the memory of everyone's smelly bare feet. The fuzzy bacteria trap also harbors everything that is spilled on it, not to mention every human byproduct under the sun, including, but not limited to, dead skin, dandruff, dried deodorant, boogers, sneezes, sleepy seeds, scabs, spit, sweat, toe jam, barf, earwax, pubes, and anything that can be projectile-launched from a baby. Thanks!

Like a tree's rings, I am certain our future culture and even extraterrestrials will study present-day living habits by analyzing the spills in our carpets. God knows they'll last longer than we will.

THE FACTS

Dr. Seymour Butts invented the hospital gown. He may have collaborated with someone else, but I assure you it was not Tim Gunn. This garment—also known as a patient gown, exam gown, or johnny shirt—is a short-sleeved, thigh-length, awkwardly sized garment worn by patients in hospitals and other medical facilities. If you have never worn one, you must be the picture of health, or perhaps have been imprisoned since birth in an Austrian basement, having never seen the light of day.

Whether worn frontward or backward, they're awkward, uncomfortable, and quite revealing.

The "better" hospital gown is made of cotton that can withstand repeated laundering in hot water and is fastened at the back with twill tape ties. However, 80 percent of hospitals now use disposable hospital gowns made of ungainly paper or thin plastic. Both suck equally.

[you] RIFE!

Mr. Butts, you stink as a designer. And, quite frankly, we must put some blame on the fashion industry too. Why hasn't someone designed something better? It seems to me that there is a lot of money to be made if every patient in every hospital needs one. And Tim Gunn, you should share the blame as well. Though few would debate that the old version looks better when worn by Heidi Klum, why have your "designers" NOT had a "challenge" where they had to create a fashion-forward hospital habit?

№047

William Harley and Arthur Davidson
For making us deaf.

THE FACTS

Harley-Davidson is an American motorcycle company that got its start at the beginning of the twentieth century. If you haven't heard of it, that's probably because loud exhaust noise has made you deaf. Many people (with the exception of a few men who really like leather) believe the two-wheeled chick magnet is a sound nuisance. I'm sure you've had a peaceful outdoor meal in the summertime ruined by a gang of hog riders cruising by.

But stories like that do not compel Harley-Davidson to quiet its ride. In fact, the Milwaukee motorcycle maker loved its uproariousness so much it even tried to trademark its loud self-proclaimed "potato-potato-potato" sound in the nineties. A battle in court with a couple of Japanese motorcycle companies lasted about six years before Harley-Davidson decided to throw in the bandana. But Harley claimed it had won in the court of public opinion anyway.

[you] RIFE!

So if you're a Harley rider, we just want you to know: You're so macho—you ma-cho ma-cho man. I'm sure you notice that everyone turns their heads when you ride by. But take a moment away from tightening up your leather chaps, wipe the exhaust from your biker goggles, and focus on their facial expressions. Aside from the one guy who is winking and lickin' his lips at you, I assure you that everyone has a look of disgust that nearly parallels the look the Speedo guy gets (see RIFE №003).

Okay, it's like a state of mind, freedom, the open road, and "screw the system" all wrapped up in an American-made grease bucket. I get it—I really do. I mean, nothing shouts liberation like shiny studded jewelry, fringe, saddlebags, and leather vests. But seriously, when you set off more car alarms than California's earthquakes, it's just too much. Ride AWAY from town and go explore your freedom on the open (dirt) road. Then, afterward, maybe you can meet up with your gang at the Blue Oyster Bar and show off your shiny tailpipes.

Insurance frauds
For making insurance rates expensive.

THE FACTS

One out of every three car crashes involving bodily injury is fraudulent.

There are many different types of insurance: auto, home, medical, life, etc. They all have one thing in common: They are susceptible to fraud. Insurance fraud has been around since the start of insurance. Even as far back as ancient Greece, people would scam "insurers" by purposefully sinking or hiding a ship to claim the insurance bounty.

[you] RIFE!

So what's the big deal? Fraudulent insurance scams raise our rates and make us victims. I agree with Ned Flanders, who thinks insurance is a form of gambling. Not to mention that you pay premiums your whole life and when you finally need it, the insurance companies haggle you on the payout. Either way you look at it, it's a dirty business. The best medicine is not to drive!

Here are the three popular car insurance scams to avoid:

- The Staged Rear-End Accident. A scammer slams on the breaks so you rear-end them. Along with collecting money for the damage, they will fake injury. Lesson learned: Never follow too closely.
- Adding Damage. A fraudulent driver adds more damage after an accident occurs to get a bigger settlement. Lesson learned: Be sure to take pictures at the scene if you are at fault.
- The Phony Wave. This is the guy who waves you on, but then crashes into you, after which he will deny waving you on to collect the insurance money. Lesson learned: Always use your best judgment in traffic.

Good luck out there!

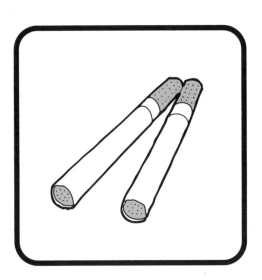

№049

Big Tobacco
For killing its customers.
(and smokers, for playing along)

THE FACTS

Cigarette smoking is the preeminent source of preventable premature deaths in the world. Smoking-related diseases cause four hundred and forty thousand American deaths each year and cost the U.S. more than $150 billion annually in health care. Cigarette smoke contains at least forty-eight hundred chemicals, sixty-nine of which are known to cause cancer . . . yada, yada, yada . . . B-O-R-I-N-G! We already know! Jesus, can we just move forward?

[you] RIFE!

Yes, cigarettes are bad for you. Yes, the tobacco companies lied. Yes, they ruined it for everybody. Yes, they are going to hell. Of course they are to blame for countless deaths, stinky breath, yellow teeth, and streets littered with butts. The only question is: Why are people still smoking? Aside from the fact that you look so cool blowing smoke like a dragon, what's the thrill? What is it? WHAT? Rebellion? Relaxation? I used to smoke to alleviate stress and to escape for a few minutes at work, but I wised up and quit. What's your status? Are you a "lifer," or are you just an unsuccessful quitter?

It's easy to blame "Big Tobacco" for promoting a deadly product. But that time is over. Accept the facts: Smoking is bad for you and we all know it. So now, it's your fault if you still smoke. If you want to quit, help is available. Get some and do it!

And by the way, if you ever hear someone say they can't quit because they're too addicted, it's bullshit. Yes, it is difficult to quit smoking. Some even claim it's more addictive than heroin. Well, have you ever seen someone detox from heroin? I can assure you, it entails a lot more than a few headaches and being a little irritable. If you want to quit, stop being a baby and throw away the coffin nails. Your loved ones will gladly stand beside you all the way (especially after you quit, because then you won't stink nearly as much).

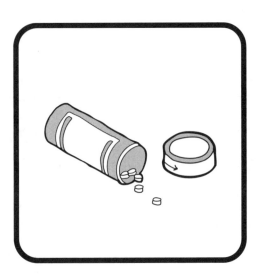

№ 050

The Consumer Product Safety Commission
For making it a headache to open aspirin.

THE FACTS

If you have found yourself looking for a hammer to finish the job after struggling with a childproof pill container, trust me, you're not alone. We have the Consumer Product Safety Commission to thank for our lid-popping problems. U.S. law has required locking mechanisms on all potentially dangerous products since 1970 for child protection.

I guess the question is: Is this necessary? I am not anti-child by any means, but how many lives is this saving? If you personally don't have any problems opening these containers, then just wait until you become elderly. Eventually, you will be shaking your cane at these hard-to-open pill bottles. Don't forget, you will have more bottles to open when you're old, and dexterity decreases with arthritis.

[you] RIFE!

When I was a toddler, I didn't even know pill containers existed. They were high up in the cabinets, a bit out of reach for a sub-three-footer. I was more into the big shiny bottles under the sink! I could reach those things easily and dump them all over the floor. Ironically, you are hard-pressed to find a pill bottle without a safety cap, but most cleaning products are a few twists or a couple squirts away from a call to poison control.

Yet the "protection" we do have just makes life more difficult. Most households rarely need safety devices like these. The CPSC obviously didn't do its job very well in the first place if it missed security on the more dangerous products. If you were really trying to protect toddlers, you would know it's easier to get into accessible cleaning products. I guess I should be careful what I wish for before someone sues the big chemical companies and padlocks become mandatory on all kitchen cabinets.

Parents should just lock up all potentially harmful things and call it a day! (Just like you would do with alcohol when your kids become teenagers.)

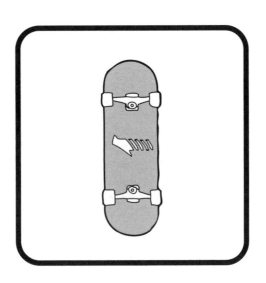

Nº051

Michael J. Fox
For causing skateboard accidents.

THE FACTS

Great Scott! *Back to the Future* is the best movie of all time. I watched it so many times in my youth, I can recite the entire movie by heart. I am sure you have seen it multiple times yourself. But in case your religion bans the viewing of PG movies, I will give you a few keywords: Michael J. Fox, the eighties, the fifties, skateboards, time machine, and 1.21 gigawatts!

Here is the only problem with the film: In the beginning, Marty McFly (Fox) is late to school. He rushes off on his skateboard and proceeds to hitch a ride on the rear bumpers of a few vehicles. He does this again toward the middle of the movie to evade his enemy, Biff. This act of being pulled behind a vehicle on a skateboard is called skitching. It was the coolest thing I had ever seen when I was ten years old. Unfortunately, it's also one of the most dangerous things you can do on a skateboard.

[you] RIFE!

I annoyingly begged my dad for an exact replica of Marty's skateboard for my birthday. Shortly after getting acclimated on it, I was determined to be like Mike! I had it planned—I would secretly grab on to the back of my mom's car on her way to the store. I did just that, and quickly lost control of the board. My fingers got stuck on the bumper and I could not let go. I was pulled half a block before I could get free. My mom had no idea, and I hobbled back in bloody shame. After she found out, I was forced, as punishment, to play in the soccer tournament the next day still severely damaged with road rash. Mr. Fox, your cool yet risky actions were not resistant enough to imitation by a die-hard fan. How many other nameless victims injured themselves in similar accidents? We blame you!

Unfortunately, my favorite childhood movie star was diagnosed with Parkinson's disease in 1991. But instead of complaining about it, he took action. The Teen Wolf has achieved great strides in Parkinson's awareness and research. You are more than forgiven for your jovial skateboard stunts. We love you. All we want to know is when Mattel's gonna start selling those hoverboards!

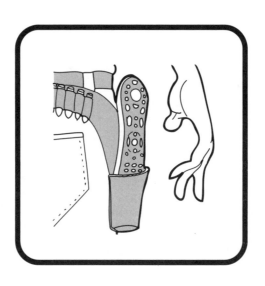

№052

Mike Ramsay and Jim Barton
For inventing TiVo.

THE FACTS

TiVo was invented by Ramsay and Barton in the late nineties. TiVo is great. If you can't afford one or don't subscribe to a DVR service, you're spending too much money on drugs. Put down the pipe, pick up the phone, and order one. When you do, you'll feel a sudden, almost overwhelming sense of freedom, similar to a pardoned death row inmate. I'm not kidding—your toes will tingle and your head will spin all the way around from excitement once you've been paired with this magical recording box. No longer do you have to rush home or fear missing your favorite programming ever again! You are free from being a slave to the inconsiderate network time slots. Channel surfing will be a thing of the past. And commercials? You will never have to hear one more "HeadOn, apply directly to the forehead" ever again!

[you] RIFE!

Take note: This perfect invention does have inevitable flaws. Pure evil will escape and fill the TV room with backhanded selfishness. The evil usually starts seeping out in mass quantities once your significant other and/or roommate discover TiVo's capabilities. Once this happens they will then turn against you.

Let's say you live with your lover, spouse, or friend and maintain a healthy relationship. As soon as you begin to share this device, put 911 on speed dial, set up a spy camera, arm yourself with dinnerware, and prepare to catch them TiVo-tampering. And beware: The TiVo can backstab its owner as well. Let's say you delete a *Gilmore Girls* rerun to make space for recording a playoff game. Remember, TiVo doesn't make mistakes; you make mistakes. And you will probably become a statistic on the domestic abuse victims list—NOT by mistake.

If TiVo starts meddling with your domestic lifestyle, I suggest you perform a séance. Break out the candles, face your palms up, and start chanting "Light as a feather, stiff as a board, we shall fight over TiVo—NO more." And remember, sharing is a good thing (unless, of course, it's a song and the music industry catches you).

№053

IBM
For inventing spell-checker.

THE FACTS

The first spell-checker was created by a group of six linguists from Georgetown University for IBM in the late seventies. The first spell-check program for a personal computer was created in 1980. From there, it became an integral part of all word-processing software. Today, even Web browsers have spell-check support that will alert you with red underlining when the smart side of your brain farts.

[you] RIFE!

Software like this makes us lazy and stupid.

Unfortunately, I am the worst abuser of this spelling aid. Okay, I will admit it: I cheated on my spelling tests as a kid. It has haunted me my entire life. The night before a test, I would press extra hard while writing the spelling words in a notebook. I would then remove the top page, revealing below a sheet of paper that had a faint imprint of the words already spelled correctly. Then I would simply use that piece of paper for the test. Quite deviant, I know.

Maybe I am to blame, 'cause people like me are the reason they invented spell-check in the first place. Maybe it's the teacher's fault for not catching me. Or, possibly, IBM is accountable for being too geeky and creating the damn thing. Either way, it's turning our heads into Jell-O. Consequently, studies have shown that if the average man were forced to compete in a one-on-one spelling bee faceoff, broccoli would win.

№054

The Yellow Pages
For wasting trees.

THE FACTS

Every year, five hundred and forty million phone directories are delivered in the United States. That's nearly two books for every American. Nineteen million trees and 7.2 billion barrels of oil are used in making these over-issued directories.

The Reuben H. Donnelley Company claims that it published the first classified telephone directory for the Chicago area around 1886. The phone book was a great tool for a long time, but most of us have moved on. Unless you need a booster seat, or you are doing experiments on *MythBusters*, they are a complete waste of trees.

Thanks to advertisements, the publishers of these nearly obsolete directories are making $14 billion yearly in the U.S. Even if the phone book becomes obsolete, these companies will surely fight hard to keep them in circulation, because they account for 97 percent of their revenues. Only 3 percent comes from online directories.

[you] RIFE!

When was the last time you actually looked up a phone number in a phone book? If you are like me, it has been years! Our world has rapidly transformed, and we use digital directories now. But for some Americans, old habits die hard. It's fine if they want to send an old-timer his big phone index, but I don't need mine anymore. So STOP sending it to me!

There is a number to call to stop the delivery of the useless yellow book. I called it and opted out, but it didn't work. They still send me two. If you like, call them to see if you can get them to stop your delivery. Hopefully you get better results. In the meantime, here are some uses for unwanted phone books: recycle it, use it as a kindling for a fireplace or campfire, shred it and use it on your garden to prevent weeds, ball it up and use it instead of peanuts for packing, make it into papier-mâché, or use it for bra stuffing to save on costly surgery.

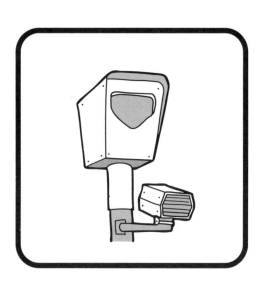

№055

Maurice Gatsonides
For inventing photo traffic citations.

THE FACTS

Maurice Gatsonides was a Dutch rally car driver who invented the speed camera in the 1950s. He originally created the device to measure cornering speed and improve his racing. Unfortunately, he chose to use his invention for evil by creating a company named Gatso and selling his sneaky equipment to law enforcement agencies. European cities use it for red light cameras and photo radar for speeding violations. Recently, many U.S. cities have embraced the "spying" technology.

If you have not seen one of these obtrusive metal contraptions near an intersection of a stop-and-go light, then DO NOT move from the town you're living in. Red light cameras are now being used in thirty cities in nineteen states.

[you] RIFE!

Studies have shown that red light cameras actually increase the number of accidents at the "enforced" intersections. The problem is that drivers who want to avoid a ticket will dangerously speed through an intersection. Also, many accidents happen because people slam on their breaks to avoid going through a yellow light for fear of a fine caused by the dreaded photo flash, which then causes rear-end collisions.

Gatso, you sold your soul! What horrible irony too: You first made your living from driving fast and dangerously, then you profit from others driving fast and dangerously illegally. You betrayed your passion, along with your fellow countrymen. You became nothing but a glorified tattletale who will be cursed and detested by ticketed victims as the anti-motor-Christ.

For those of you with a lead foot who have trouble keeping the speedometer at the double-nickel, keep an eye out for potential speed cameras in the future. And cameras, why don't you make yourself useful by photographing men shaving and women putting on makeup while driving? (You know who you are.)

№056

Overprotective parents
For ruining children.

THE FACTS

There are roughly forty million children between five and fourteen years old in the U.S. About one hundred and thirty die every year from riding a bike. That is 0.0003 percent. To put things into perspective, your odds of getting struck by lighting are 0.0002 percent. So basically, the odds of a child dying due to *not* wearing a helmet are slim to none. Also, the odds of your child being stolen in a non-custody-related child abduction are about one in a million. Your kid is one hundred times more likely to have a genius IQ. It's time to stop hovering. Lay off constantly giving instruction. Quit ruling out activities based on a danger factor. Not wearing a condom is dangerous and you still did that! You cannot protect children from everything, so STOP overdoing it! Worrying too much can have negative consequences.

[you] RIFE!

Overprotective parents are ruining our children's futures. Parents today are taking physical and emotional protection of their kids too far. I am neither promoting neglect nor am I discouraging helmets. I am, however, advocating healthy mental growth in our youth. Don't teach children to fear failure. Sometimes kids must fall and hurt themselves to learn what not to do. If you never experience failure in what you are bad at, you will never feel accomplishment in what you do well. Nobody is good at everything. Yes, they will cry, and yes, they will bleed. This is called CHARACTER. Allow them to build it, because one day (believe it or not) they will have to function on their own.

Here are a few things the older generations survived just fine: no helmets, no cell phones, no childproof containers, no antibacterial wipes, rides in the back of pickup tucks, shared drinks, eating paint, eating sugar, going to the store alone, breaking bones without filing lawsuits, eating worms, playing with firecrackers, and staying out past dark while still making it home alive.

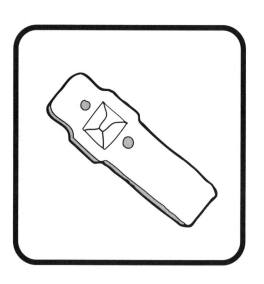

№057

Jack Welch
For security tag false alarms.

THE FACTS

Jack Welch invented the annoying beeping you frequently encounter at the entrance/exit of your favorite store. He didn't invent the sound; he just created the device that triggers the noise. Jack, along with his cousin, invented and produced the noisy antitheft device in the 1960s. Little did they know that they would be creating the world's most worthless security device (well, second only to the car alarm). Their company still leads the electronic security market worldwide. They sell over a billion dollars' worth of the noisy anti-shoplifting tags every year, although I don't understand why store owners waste their time with these ineffective devices.

Take note of what really happens the next time one of these buzzers goes off. Once the alarm sounds, if a clerk even turns his head, be surprised. Usually, nobody will. If someone does, they will glance for a quick racial profiling and see if you look like a thief. Then, if you don't run or impersonate Winona, they'll probably just wave you on.

[you] RIFE!

Thanks for nothing, Jack. I am sure we would give praise if you had actually invented something that worked! As far as I can tell, this POS just creates a lot of noise and frustration. Cell phones and purchased clothing with metal strips sewn in account for most of the false alarms.

Maybe this device works in theory, but the execution sucks. The problem is fueled by user error—employees don't remove tags and forget to demagnetize the strips.

The excessive amount of false alarms has desensitized us. The alarm should go off only when an item is being stolen, with NO exceptions. Remember, the best theft deterrent is fear, the fear of being caught and the fear of punishment. Maybe it's time we started cutting off fingers! Or even worse, locking shoplifters up in white padded rooms with the security device alarms blaring for a couple of days. Ah . . . the sweet sound of justice.

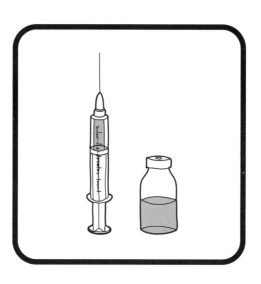

Alex Rodriguez
For teaching children it's okay to cheat.

THE FACTS

Alex Rodriguez is the highest-paid ballplayer in Major League Baseball. He has played ball for the Texas Rangers, the Seattle Mariners, and the New York Yankees. Many believe him to be one of the best players of all time. He is also the youngest player to hit five hundred home runs. It's quite amazing how far he can whack that white ball with the red stitching. However, it has come to light that he had a little help from a "friend."

In response to the revelation of his steroid use, Alex stated, "I'm guilty for a lot of things. I'm guilty for being negligent, naive, not asking all the right questions . . . To be quite honest, I don't know exactly what substance I was guilty of using." Spare us. You knew exactly what you were doing and exactly what you were taking.

[you] RIFE!

Poor little A-Rod. You are just a victim, boohoo. We all feel so sorry for you and the pressures society has put on you. Oh—wait a minute . . . you cheated your way to the top by taking performance-enhancing drugs. No—we don't feel sorry for you—AT ALL. We should start issuing a no-tolerance law for this sort of bullshit.

Some say he wasn't hurting anybody, only himself. You know, he didn't train dogs to kill other dogs, or rape some underage girls or intentionally injure another player. Screw that! He was our hero and he lied. It's not okay to break the rules. He taught our children it's okay to cheat your way to the top! This is their idol? Great role model, A-hole. And worst of all, you're still allowed to play. Hey, A-Rod, hopefully you can right this wrong and do some good in your life. Maybe tour high schools teaching sports safety and how to hit the right vein?

I'm sick of all of the "asterisks" that keep popping up in the record books. It's disappointing for the ballplayers who played it straight. Here are some "top" players we should denounce for their alleged drug use: Barry Bonds, Roger Clemens, Mark McGwire, Rafael Palmeiro, and Jose Canseco. Since you weren't sacked from baseball—you're fired from being our heroes.

№059

The automatic-flush toilet inventor
For a cockamamie idea.

THE FACTS

I am not even going to waste my time looking up who invented this worthless contraption.

[you] RIFE!

Everyone poops—it's a fact of life. Every household and business has at least one toilet. It's a big industry. There's a lot of money to be made in the disposal of human excrement. Unfortunately, there's not much room for improvement. But of course some idiot had to go and ruin a good thing.

Many public restrooms now have auto-flush commodes and urinals. The only benefit to the auto-flush toilet is sanitation, but it's nothing a simple hand washing (which everyone should be doing after dropping the kids off at the pool) can't fix.

The negatives certainly outweigh the barely positive. Auto-flushing never seems to work when it's supposed to. There's no opportunity to either pre-flush or courtesy flush. It's scary for small children. If it flushes too often, water is wasted. If it works too little, it's unsanitary. There's just too much room for error, especially when a highly effective foot or hand lever will do the trick.

If you think the toilet-seat lever is the dirtiest thing in your day, think again. The door handles to the stall and bathroom door are usually dirtier. If the inventor wanted to get anal with the lavatory experience, he should have created an automatic door opener. Here are some other things usually dirtier than a toilet: a cell phone, a keyboard, a mouse, a faucet, a kitchen sponge, a purse, a wallet, money, and makeup.

With that said, just how clean are you? It takes about twenty seconds of washing to get your hands germ-free. When was the last time you did that?

No060

Photoshop
For tricking us into online dating.

THE FACTS

Adobe Photoshop is a photo-editing software application used for many things, including photo altering and enhancing. Every single picture you see in a magazine was altered in some way to look better than it really is, usually through Photoshop. Unfortunately, a law preventing overembellishment while using this type of software has not been passed. Now the online dating community is flooded with suspiciously enhanced and/or modified photos.

Just look at some of these dating and social networking sites. These people are HOT! The not-so-fine line between enticement and porn has been crossed. It's basically soft-core smut. Check it out. Forty million Americans already do!

[you] RIFE!

If you're single and looking, you'll soon find that there aren't many social outlets to search for a soul mate. I mean, you can always try flowers or a compliment like "You smell nice," but in today's nonsocial environment you will probably be served with a sexual harassment suit. You could also ask your friends to set you up with someone, but only if you are interested in burning a bridge or two. Or maybe you're old-fashioned and you want to take your chances at a bar. Guess again: If you're a dude, you only have a 2 percent chance of any relationship ever happening there. Ready to give up? Well, hold on . . . there is one choice left . . . It's called online dating. This can be a viable solution—BUT BE WARNED: Photoshop has made it tricky. You now have to look at photos of people who might not be as hot as their pictures may appear. There is really no way of knowing if a smudge on a forehead isn't really just a post-edited third eye. And here's the kicker: Why do we have such high expectations to begin with? It's because the magazine covers are ALSO being Photoshopped. You bastards!

Here are some online dating photo don'ts (from a man's perspective):

• Ditch the photo of you and your dog. Do I even have to explain?
• Black-and-white photos are not allowed. Don't use them unless you're Rita Hayworth.
• Get rid of photos with friends. Unless you're suggesting what I think you're suggesting.

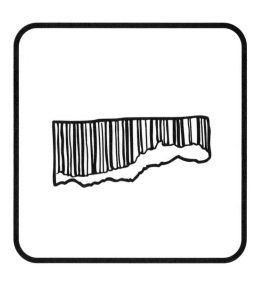

Nº061

R. Stanton Avery
For leaving a sticky residue.

THE FACTS

In 1935, R. Stanton Avery manufactured the first self-adhesive label (a.k.a. the sticker). It had a paper surface with a coat of adhesive that peeled from a silicone backing and stuck to just about anything. Today, stickers can be found on almost every consumer product we buy.

It's not the sticker that upsets most people. It's the removal of it! And the sticky residue marring your brand new purchase.

[you] RIFE!

Enough is enough. Life is complicated already without the added grief of having to remove this gooey crap from everything we buy. Lately, it seems retailers have become even more sticker crazy. I want a refund on my time! If you want to make it come off in a few pieces so shoplifters won't be able to reassemble it onto a more expensive item, then do it. But for fuck's sake, use easily peeling adhesive.

I have tried everything to remove this stuff: WD-40, a hair dryer, Scotch tape, razor blades, rubbing alcohol, lighter fluid, even profusely cursing at it. However, nothing seems to work. The most successful way to get rid of the sticker is to simply throw the entire product in the dumpster. Once it is trash, it becomes someone else's problem, and then you can sigh with relief.

Here is a list of other things that are annoyingly impossible to remove: pine tree sap, magic marker, wax, bubble gum, buffalo wing sauce under fingernails, salmon smell, the lid on old maple syrup, wrinkles, oil-based paint, scratches on the new car, wine stains, orange patina from Cheetos, purple-sucker tongue, safety info on car sun visors, loud neighbors, hair, funnily shaped moles, cancer, acne, and most politicians.

For ruining immune system development.

THE FACTS

Is there such a thing as too clean?

Ever wonder why they tell you not to drink the water in Mexico? Mexicans seem unfazed by drinking their H_2O. It's because your body has not built up an immunity to the extra germs in their water. Germs are what STRENGTHEN an immune system. The more you encounter at a young age, the more your body will learn to fight them off. Take note, I am not telling you to go lick your nearest gas station commode. I am, however, telling you to stop overdoing it with the antibacterial stuff.

Believe it or not, most bacteria out there are serving a good purpose.

[you] RIFE!

Germaphobes are ruining the development of our children's immune systems. Parents think they are doing the right thing by overprotecting their kin from bacteria. However, we need these bacteria for proper development. Just like children need exercise for strong bones and muscles, they need germs to build a healthy resistance to infections. This includes being exposed to allergens ranging from dust to pollen to cat dander.

It's believed that antibacterial soaps promote super-resistant BAD bacteria. Not to mention these harsh cleansers destroy GOOD bacteria as well. Good bacteria are vital for digestion, germ fighting, making vitamins, and protecting our skin.

But don't throw away your antibacterial gels and soaps just yet. Use them when someone at work or home gets diagnosed with a flesh-eating disease or when a pandemic is in effect. Also, you can do other things to fight bacteria, such as avoiding using the same towel for drying your hands over and over (this is one of those bad-bacteria traps). And seriously, don't drink the water in Mexico.

№063

The U.S. Department of Agriculture
For inventing the four food groups.

THE FACTS

Since 1894, the USDA has been developing and redeveloping the dietary food standards for the American people. It's the agency that suggests what we should eat and how much. Ever hear of the food pyramid? Thank the USDA. Once upon a time, the USDA even stuffed all of our food into four groups. I mean, it was quite profound, especially since there used to be twelve groups around. It even made one group just dairy, and then forgot to categorize the Bloody Mary . . .

[you] RIFE!

Are you hungry? I am—damn. Damn, I am! And I do not like that USDA scam!
I would not like it here, I would not like it there, I would not like it anywhere!
It doesn't even have a group for Spam, and I like my Spam. It makes me hungry. Damn, I am!

After the four-group-to-pyramid switch, we found choosing food to be a bitch.
Do we eat a tasty fox, or add mustard to a cardboard box?
This whole thing's just too confusing. And it's not weight that we're losing!
Hey! USDA. One day you'll pay. If not today, then soon, with little delay!

Sorry . . . I went off on a tangent there. I can't just end this RIFE on pabulum poems . . . Did you ever wonder what happened to the "Basic Four" food groups? Well, actually, through the years the USDA has gone from five, to twelve, to seven, to four, and back to five food groups. And then it made some generic pyramid. I'm sure it has some scientific reasoning, but the USDA changes its nutrition rules faster than most fad dieters. The system has become so confusing and depressing, it makes you want to eat only cheeseburgers. It doesn't separate different types of proteins, suggests all complex carbs are good, thinks all fats are bad, doesn't mention vitamins, and forgets to recommend exercise. Hope your dinner guest is Tom Hanks: Maybe he can help you decipher the food code! Now the USDA has a personalized "My Pyramid" scheme to complicate things more. But I think it's all a scam. Check and see . . . Soon you'll be yelling— LET ME BE!

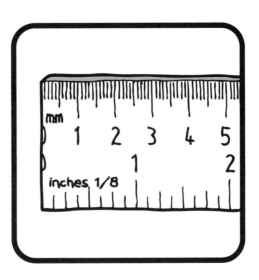

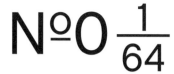

The imperial system of measurement
For not going away.

THE FACTS

The imperial system of measurement is a system of units based on a nearly one-thousand-year-old measuring standard. Its ideology is based on nature and everyday activities, NOT science. The imperial system originated in the U.K., which in turn lent it to the U.S. But differences were acquired over time. For example, the U.S. measuring system's pint has sixteen ounces, and the version in England has twenty ounces. (Does that mean you will be more lightheaded if you donate a pint of blood in England?)

With the exception of the United States, all major countries have converted to the metric system. How is this possible? Oh, wait a minute, we are talking about the United States—land of the free, home of the pigheaded. While the U.S. has attempted to switch, unsuccessfully, in the past, we nevertheless march on with the inferior and confusing system.

[you] RIFE!

Imperial system, please go away. You are outdated and have no relevance in modern society. You should be hung out to dry like your old buddy Latin. The system was created by farmers one thousand years ago and it's much more difficult to learn. Hell, just converting units is enough to give a student Tourette syndrome. The advantages of the metric system are clear: It's a modern system based on scientific principles. There are only seven basic measurements. It's easy to understand, because all the units in the metric system are multiples of ten. It's smart and has relevance in today's society. Which seems more logical to you?

  a) Metric system: 1 meter = 10 decimeters = 100 centimeters = 1,000 millimeters.
  b) Imperial system: 1 yard = 3 feet = 12 inches = various fractions of an inch.

We are in a digital-viewing, nano-researching, space-exploring, and technological era. Come on, America, it is time to get rid of a measurement based on some dead king's stinky foot.

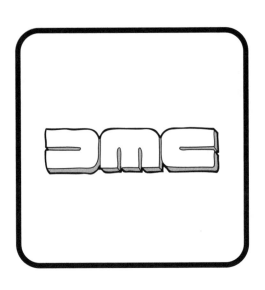

№065

John DeLorean
For producing only one car . . . sniff, sniff.

THE FACTS

John DeLorean was an American automobile engineer. A former GM exec well known for developing the Pontiac GTO and the Firebird, DeLorean was obsessed with the idea of creating his dream car, one that was "fun to drive, safe to operate, and long-lasting." His eponymous DeLorean DCM-12 was first produced in 1981 and had a unique stainless steel finish with gull-wing-style flip-up doors. DeLorean came as close as anyone to successfully challenging the three overly powerful American carmakers. At the time, General Motors, Chrysler, and Ford were all shaking in their safety-buckles over actually having some American competition. On top of that, the car's fame, and DeLorean's own, were later catapulted into the stratosphere when the DCM-12 was immortalized as our favorite time machine (see RIFE №051).

Unfortunately, none of this would change the car industry the way it should have. The entrepreneur hit financial turmoil shortly after getting his company off the ground. And what, may you ask, does a venturesome car company owner do when he runs out of money? . . . He sells drugs.

Undercover federal agents proposed a drug trafficking deal to DeLorean that would supposedly bring in millions to save his business. In 1982, the industrialist was arrested by the U.S. government for trafficking cocaine.

[you] RIFE!

John, you sold out to drug dealing and lost your car company. You couldn't raise any more venture capital the legal way? People revered the car; if you asked for more money, they would have invested. You had a good thing going with the DeLorean Motor Company. I'm confident the auto industry would be different today if DMC continued with its innovations.

Of course, the feds are to blame too. John DeLorean was found NOT guilty due to entrapment. The FBI simply persuaded a desperate man to commit an act he would not have otherwise considered. Great detective work, guys!

Well, John, you gave a new meaning to the term car "dealer." Rest in peace knowing, if given the chance, in today's turmoil, the Big Three automakers would be more than happy to profit from a little booger sugar.

№666

Pope Siricius
For being the devil in disguise.

THE FACTS

Pope Siricius was pope from 384 to 399 AD. He was the guy who started the whole no-sex-for-clergy thing. But take note, he wasn't exactly a purist. He was married, and then left his wife for the church. So basically, the Catholic Church promoted him for getting a divorce? Interesting.

In 1985, sexual abuse by a Catholic priest became a national issue in the United States for the first time. Gilbert Gauthe, a priest from Louisiana, pleaded guilty to eleven counts of molestation of boys. He admitted to molesting at least three dozen more. They gave him twenty years. He got out in ten. Then he got in trouble again. Unfortunately, these cases are not uncommon. It's time for sex-offender sentencing to include a lobotomy.

Four percent of U.S. priests ministering from 1950 to 2002 were accused of sex abuse with a minor. Roman Catholics spent $615 million on sex abuse cases in 2007—remember that when you place a dollar in the collection tray.

[you] RIFE!

Did these "holy" sex offenders forget to ask themselves, "WWJD?" Seriously, can we ever trust our children with a priest again? Pope Siricius not only ruined it for priests, but more importantly, he ruined it for the altar boys. As for Gilbert, you are one sick puppy. How you made it out of jail alive is beyond me. A priest used to be a figure of respect and trust, but no more. Gilbert surely sacrificed that.

The Catholic Church's halo isn't exactly shining all that brightly either. For years, it swept cases like these under its Roman tapestries. If a priest was caught, the church would slap him on the wrist and just transfer him to a different parish (where he would usually commit the same ungodly acts). Gauthe was transferred three times before he was finally brought to justice. It's time for a change! Seriously, nobody is going to call a priest unholy if he gets married. At least promote promiscuity between priests and nuns so they can release some holy sexual tension! As for Catholic followers, be extra suspicious if your priest drives a windowless van.

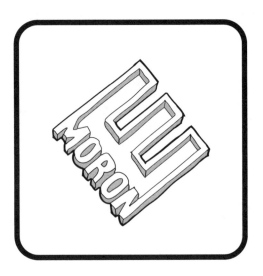

№ 067

THE FACTS

Enron started as an energy company. It dabbled in many investment areas and rapidly grew to be the seventh-largest corporation in America. Then it quickly folded in what became one of the biggest scandals of fraud and greed in history. Its bankruptcy took jobs, investor savings, retirement funds, and even a few lives. Now no one can ever really feel secure with his or her employer ever again.

Enron achieved great success the old-fashioned way—by cheating. The company paid out millions of dollars in speculated profits that never arrived. The energy giant hid its losses by burying its debt into ghost companies it created. Then it paid off outside accountants to lie about its tax audits. And just before Enron tanked, its top executives liquidated their holdings while conning their loyal employees into holding on to the doomed stock. The head honchos made off with BAGS of cash while the employees and investors lost billions.

[you] RIFE!—All of you!

- Ken Lay: CEO and chairman of Enron. He was a forerunner of deregulation, which ultimately paved an easy path for his corporate abuses. He was found guilty of conspiracy and fraud. Unfortunately, he died before we could send him up the river.
- Jeff Skilling: He started the mark-to-market accounting that gave access to money made on speculation. Well, now he can speculate if he's next on Bubba's prison-bitch list, because he's currently rotting in jail.
- Arthur Andersen: This was the "independent" accounting firm hired to review Enron's books to protect the public. But nope, they took bribes and cooked the books.
- The politicians: Both political parties had their hands in Enron's deep pockets. And if we asked for a show of those hands, George W.'s administration would raise both.
- The consultants: Enron's lawyers, accountants, bankers, and advisers all knew it was a scam. They just kept their mouths shut and collected their kickbacks.
- Enron employees: You guys lost so much it's hard to blame you too—but we will anyway. Were sunglasses and canes part of your work-issued uniforms? It is amazing just how powerful denial can be. Want your money back? Turn the CEOs' lawyers upside down and start shaking!

№068

Scott Boras and Drew Rosenhaus
For ruining professional sports.

THE FACTS

Remember Bob Sugar in the film *Jerry Maguire*? He was the asshole sports agent who stole Jerry's clients. Well, Drew Rosenhaus is the real-life Bob Sugar. In fact, the character was based on him. Make no mistake, Rosenhaus is a real-deal high-profile sports agent. He represents many NFL superstars. He's an aggressive negotiator who drives up the prices and gets athletes ridiculous salaries. Similarly, Scott Boras is another notorious sports agent. His clients are baseball players. He is known as "baseball's most hated man." Boras also gets unheard-of deals for his clients. As a result, these deals usually hurt Major League Baseball by widening the gap between wealthy and poor teams.

[you] RIFE!

You greedy dicks. Here is the rundown: They get the high-profile players huge sums of money, which alienates them from the average professional player. The problem is, the big names already get multi-million-dollar endorsement deals anyway. Are they really increasing a star's quality of living by negotiating an extra six million when they already make five? Or are they just worried about increasing their commissions? All they are really doing is raising our ticket prices, and, of course, just like Charlie Sheen's love life, we pay for it.

What is throwing a ball through a hoop worth? What is the cost of seeing someone whack a ball with a wooden stick or kick a ball into a net? Is it equal to someone saving a life? How about educating a child? Or fighting for others' freedom? We really need to rethink who the heroes are, and how they should be rewarded. Teachers, doctors, and firemen should be our heroes. Perhaps they are noble because they follow their hearts to do the right thing, all for shitty pay. Or maybe they are selling themselves short. Perhaps they should seek agent sponsorship. Give Scott or Drew a call and see what kind of contract they can fetch for you . . .

In defense of the accused, Rosenhaus did once save the life of a young boy who nearly drowned by administering CPR to him. There might still be a spot for you at the Pearly Gates after all (but don't hold your breath).

№069 | **Monica Lewinsky**
For sucking.

THE FACTS

"I'm going to the White House to get my presidential knee pads," were the inevitable words uttered by Monica Lewinsky to a friend before leaving for her internship. In case you missed the nineties, she wore those knee pads right down to the bone. She had an eighteen-month fling with Bill Clinton that involved oral and phone sex. Their actions nearly took down a good U.S. president and permanently rubber-stamped his career with the words SEX SCANDAL.

[you] RIFE!

Monica, you were such a sucker (no, the other kind—get your head out of the gutter). Did you really think the president of the United States was in love with you? Let's be realistic. But actually, the scandal wasn't entirely your fault. You just gave the nobber. Your attention-seeking hobgoblin friend Linda Tripp was the one who spilled the beans.

Okay, fine, you wanted to blow a president. That makes sense; I'm sure every young girl has dreams. So congratulations, you did it. But you should've just wiped your chin and kept your mouth shut! Next time wait until his term is up before showing off your oval rug burns to your friends. Well, anyway—we're not mad anymore. What's done is done. Besides, we are angrier about having to look at you in that stupid beret you wore on the cover of *Time* magazine.

And now everyone thinks Clinton getting his knob shined by a pudgy, patriotic vixen distracted us from his goodness. But take a moment and look at his legislation—was he good or was he just protecting his own interests?

- The Brady Bill. It's the five-day handgun waiting period. Clinton probably passed that one just to protect his own hide from angry boyfriends and husbands.
- The Three Strikes and You're Out policy. A good piece of legislation—but I think that was just a typo on a leaked memo to Monica. It should've read: Three BITES and You're Out.
- The Safe Drinking Water Act. We all know how thirsty one gets after suckin' on a cigar.
- The Direct Loan Program. It was good for funding higher education. But what it comes down to is this—he just wanted his interns better educated on the theory that loose lips sink dicks.

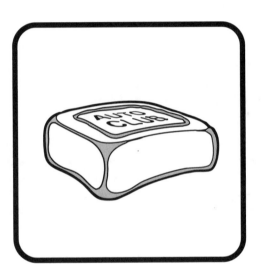

Tyler Durden
For questioning the safety of our cars.

THE FACTS

Fight Club is a movie starring Ed Norton and Brad Pitt based on the novel written by Chuck Palahniuk. This movie is clever, exciting, and fun. A total guy flick that girls love too. The plot is witty and extremely well acted. Ed Norton plays the narrator, an automobile recall appraiser. In a small part of the movie, he reveals, in detail, the equation used to assess the potential of a car recall. Ed Norton's character explains, "You take the population of vehicles in the field (A) and multiply it by the probable rate of failure (B), then multiply the result by the average cost of an out-of-court settlement (C). A times B times C equals X. This is what it will cost if we don't initiate a recall. If X is greater than the cost of a recall, we recall the cars and no one gets hurt. If X is less than the cost of a recall, then we DON'T recall."

[you] RIFE!

Thanks for that tidbit of information. Now every time we travel by car, we can never fully trust the safety of our vehicles. Just that slight doubt will always screw with our subconscious. Unfortunately, after a little research, I found the equation to be true.

In 1970, Ford introduced the Pinto. It was a subcompact designed to compete with foreign carmakers. During production, problems were found in the gas tank assembly. The fuel tank was weak and, in the event of a rear-end collision, would leak and easily ignite. Unfortunately, the human body wasn't built Ford tough, which resulted in many fiery deaths. Of course, Ford was aware of the defect and could have retooled the Pinto's design during production, but it chose not to. The auto giant could have issued a recall after cars started exploding, but it didn't allow that either. Instead, Ford did the math and decided it would be cheaper to pay the potential lawsuits.

How much is your life worth? Given Ford's estimated out-of-court settlements for death in 1970, it's around $200,000.

№071

Sony's Betamax
For starting format wars.

THE FACTS

Sony has produced a lot of great products over the last few decades. The company has had some major flops too, Betamax being the most famous (although the MiniDisc player was a close second). In this decade-long battle, JVC's VHS won the format race. But why? Beta came out first and was actually superior in quality compared to its competition.

Beta failed mostly because of its short recording time, a measly one hour at first. People wanted to record movies and football games, and this just wouldn't cut it. Eventually, Sony would extend the play time, but Beta always trailed VHS. The inferior product also failed to win consumers over because of Sony's awful marketing, bad design, and high price point.

But let's get to the key factor behind VHS's victory—porn was not available on Betamax.

[you] RIFE!

Sony had to ruin it by not fighting hard enough to win over the consumer (and for being too goody-goody about the smut videos). Of course, the real losers here are all the chumps who didn't buy VHS in the first place. It was quite a costly transition to make (especially since the DVD craze came shortly after). And of course, every consumer would eventually be hit by the wave of similarly snide technology companies that continually change platforms and media players just because they can.

So don't worry, Sony isn't shedding a tear; it's back on top with Blu-ray. Which, of course, means you will soon have to update that tired old DVD collection you spent years building. It just goes to show that in a battle versus technology, you will always lose. What does this mean for the future? Due to changing formats, you will have to repurchase the Beatles' "White Album" at least six more times in your life.

№072

Car alarm users
For making a lot of noise.

THE FACTS

A car is stolen every twenty-six seconds in the United States. Cars are easy to steal; they even have a built-in getaway system. The odds of your car being stolen are one in two hundred. You have a 13 percent chance of getting your car back. On average, the authorities are called to the scene only 1 percent of the time when a car alarm is triggered.

An educated guess would all but guarantee a car's (false) alarm is blaring somewhere in your town with no one thinking of stealing it. Rather than theft, you have a greater chance of vandalism happening to your door in the shape of someone's annoyed boot print.

[you] RIFE!

You can't blame the inventor for this one: The product performs as advertised. A car alarm won't promise the security of your car; it only guarantees that it will make a lot of annoying noise if someone ever tries to jack it (and plenty more times when a garbage truck rumbles by). The liability on this one goes to everyone who still uses car alarms. They so don't work. They just make an irritating racket and give people headaches. It has gotten to the point where everyone just tunes them out. Here is an idea: Why not make a silent alarm that alerts your phone and gives GPS coordinates when a thief steals your car? Then an iPhone app could automatically pop up and give an "Electrocute or Eject?" option. Something more like David Hasselhoff's old ride. This way you may actually be able to get your car back and then catch, prosecute, AND have some fun with the car thief.

Here are more effective car theft deterrent systems to try before you buy KITT from NBC:

- Kill switch
- LoJack
- An empty gas tank
- A chauffeur
- Snipers
- Or just stop paying your parking tickets and the police will attach the ultimate antitheft device—*the boot.*
- And if none of this works, just take the bus!

№ 073

Asbestos companies
For making our lungs biohazard sites.

THE FACTS

Asbestos is a naturally occurring mineral. There is no doubt that asbestos is a great building material. It has incredible heat resistance, which makes it flame-retardant. It has wonderful insulating properties. As long as it does not enter your lungs, there's no problem. Unfortunately, prolonged inhalation exposure, usually with individuals working in the factories that manufacture the product, will result in extreme health problems, most prominently terminal cancer.

In 1951, asbestos companies (having control over both the experiments and the printing of asbestos-related studies) removed all references to cancer before allowing their self-sponsored research to be made public. A year later a medical director at the building-insulation company Johns Manville attempted to force asbestos companies, including his own, to place a warning label on all of their products to reduce the risk of disease in workers. However, the massive companies ignored his efforts, and it took a continued loss of life for the public to find out the truth.

[you] RIFE!

As the saying goes, "Those who do not study history are doomed to repeat it." The ancient Greeks used asbestos for tablecloths and clothing because they could be cleaned in fire and would not burn. But since there was such a high demand for large-sized doilies and sear-proof panties, many slaves who worked with asbestos became deathly ill from the same health problems of the modern era. Unfortunately, there was no Wikipedia in the 1950s for easy research. As a result, people died.

You asbestos companies lucked out. Big Tobacco took a lot of smoke away from your product. As I see it, they killed their consumers and you killed your employees. But at least Big Tobacco provided some enjoyment for their stooges. You just put people in non-habit-forming hospital beds. But you both knew the harmful effects of your products and still peddled your deadly wares. You might as well have handed out fiberglass-flavored cotton candy to kids. I hope the cost of your soul was worth it, 'cause you'll be ridin' shotgun straight down with your tobacco-shilling friends.

№074

Dr. Robert Atkins
For a stupid diet.

THE FACTS

The Atkins Diet plan is a low-carb, high-protein strategy for shedding unwanted pounds, made popular in the early 2000s. About thirty million Americans have tried the diet. If you haven't heard of it, maybe you're that kid in the news who can only eat six foods without dying?

Here's the skinny: When you cut out carbohydrates, your body is forced to burn its fat stores. You burn more calories when your body burns fat as opposed to carbs. In turn, you lose weight faster.

Sounds too good to be true, right? Well, that's because it is. Short-term effects may include bad breath, weakness, insomnia, nausea, and constipation. Potential long-term effects include heart disease, liver failure, kidney problems, osteoporosis, premature aging, and cataracts. Keep in mind, the inventor, Dr. Atkins, died at seventy-two. He had a history of heart attacks and congestive heart failure. Not to mention he weighed two hundred and fifty-eight pounds at the time of his death. In case you were wondering, toast won! Thank God this no-carb bullshit is over.

[you] RIFE!

Dr. Atkins, we all really wanted to believe your diet worked. But deep down we all knew there had to be something wrong with a diet that labeled nutritious foods like fruit and whole grains the devil. After all, a slice of bacon can't be healthier than an apple. Right? You ruined it for sure. Now we have to get back to the old way of thinking: "You are what you eat." Oink oink.

Chew on this, America: Enough food is produced in the U.S. to supply thirty-eight hundred calories every day for every man, woman, and child. The average adult only needs two thousand to twenty-five hundred calories per day.

Do you want to lose weight? Then stop eating so much! Eat small, healthy meals, exercise regularly, and avoid piggin' out. And then guess what? You WILL lose weight. If you don't, then just get your stomach stapled.

№075

Phil Gramm
For legalizing deregulation.

THE FACTS

Remember that dick, Dick Fuld, from RIFE №029, and the douche bags from №067? Without the guy you're about to read about, *none* of them would have been able to screw up our lives. Phil Gramm served as chairman of the Senate Banking Committee in the late nineties. He was a proponent of financial deregulation. He wrote and pushed through Congress the Gramm-Leach-Bliley Act, which effectively repealed much of the Glass-Steagall Act. The Glass-Steagall Act was enacted as a result of the Great Depression. It separated commercial banks from Wall Street to prevent lending, use of credit, and investing by the same entity. Sort of a checks and balances for Wall Street. That all went to shit when Gramm added a provision to the Commodity Futures Modernization Act of 2000 that kept credit-default swaps exempt from government regulation. These acts of deregulation have crippled America and are major factors in the 2008-2009 banking and economic crisis.

[you] RIFE!

Your deregulation ruined it for everyone. You supplied a springboard for the greediest professions to commit fraud and make stupid mistakes. You took down the world's economy. You owe America AT LEAST a couple trillion. So break out your checkbook, you ass hat. And, it better be FDIC-insured.

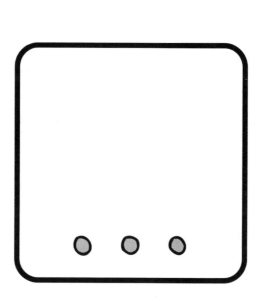

№076

MLA Handbook
For changing the spacing after a sentence.

THE FACTS

MLA stands for Modern Language Association. If you are unfamiliar with it, perhaps you are illiterate. Anyway, the *MLA Handbook for Writers of Research Papers* is an academic documentation style guide widely used in the United States and Canada. The updated version of the handbook redefines the proper spacing required at the end of a sentence. The rules have changed since the day of the typewriter; we are no longer required to have two spaces after a sentence.

What can I say, old habits die hard. I still struggle with single spacing daily. My hand just wants to hit that long bar twice after a sentence ends. Some people think the extra space is worse than having a front tooth missing from a person's smile. Apparently, the gap after a period is already accounted for with the "kerning" (which is just a fancy way of saying "spacing"). The extra distance used to make sense when every character took up an equal amount of space. Now all current word processing software automatically adjusts for the extra bit after a period.

[you] RIFE!

To be honest, it was easier for me to quit smoking than to consistently add just one thumb tap after a period.

Mostly, it's die-hard writers and publishers who want to follow the most current rules that create the dilemma. The *MLA Handbook* states that either one or two spaces are acceptable. I say, let's keep it the old way out of respect! And, quite frankly, if you noticed how many spaces I have been using thus far, you are probably not paying attention to what I am writing anyway!

I think the whole thing is a big waste of time. We should never have changed the rule in the first place. Two spaces after a sentence makes the text more readable anyway. So from here on out, I will be double-spacing just because it looks cooler. Boo-ya, MLA! I am going medieval typewriter on your ass. (Just kidding—my editor won't let me do that.)

№ 077

Blue star LSD warnings
For being a stupid urban legend.

THE FACTS

A blue star warning is a rumor spread around a community regarding lick-on acid-laced tattoos. The story is that a local drug dealer is on the prowl, handing out LSD to young children. The urban legend got its name because acid was supposedly being distributed invisibly on a small lick-on tattoo in the shape of a blue star. The threat is that a juvenile will lick the tattoo before applying it. This would then result in a psychedelic acid trip, or, worse, death. These worrisome rumors are usually started in the fall during back-to-school time. Then, of course, they die down to make way for poisoned Halloween candy rumors (see RIFE №010).

[you] RIFE!

If we had to blame somebody for this folklore, it would be J. O'Donnell of Danbury Hospital's Outpatient Chemical Dependency Clinic. This is the name usually associated with the warnings. However, since this is a fake person, we have to blame credulous parents.

As soon as gullible people hear the mention of harm to children, they would prefer self-immolation to allowing a threat like this to harm innocent, unwitting youths. Rest assured, it's horseshit. There have never been any verified cases of LSD-laced tattoos. There is, though, such a thing as cartoons printed on LSD-soaked blotter paper, which is ingested. However, nobody is giving them out to children for free. Think about it. Selling drugs is a business. It is an illegal business, but a business nonetheless. Why the hell would a drug dealer want to kill his customers before making any money off of them? The tobacco companies would be bankrupt if they followed this business model. A profitable business strategy in drug dealing would be to get customers hooked, and then keep them alive as long as possible to maximize profits. Unfortunately, a drug dealer's clientele do not need to be tricked or have freebies doled out to them; peer pressure and curiosity are more than enough.

Talk to your children and make them aware of drugs. And as a rule of thumb, take the age you were when you experimented with drugs and divide that by two, and that is the age when your child will do it.

№078

The Food and Drug Administration
For making healthy food unhealthy.

THE FACTS

The Food and Drug Administration (FDA or USFDA) is an agency of the United States Department of Health and Human Services. It's responsible for regulating and supervising the safety of foods and a bunch of other things that humans shove in their mouths and plaster on their bodies. For the most part, the FDA is here to protect us from the "bad guys." But once you give something a little power, it'll always hunger for more.

If you took a "raw" almond pre-2007, planted it the ground, watered it, and gave it sunlight and love, you would eventually see a sprout rise. If you did that now, you would get more rise out of Nicole Kidman's eyebrows. This is because ALL almonds grown in the U.S., by law, are NO longer sold raw. They must be pasteurized before they can be sold. In case you didn't already know, this process kills the life force and the valuable nutrients your body needs.

[you] RIFE!

Okay, I know we've already covered the orange juice pasteurization conspiracy—so maybe we should just blame Louis Pasteur already for inventing it in the 1860s. But he lived in a time when you couldn't exactly seal in freshness with Ziploc bags and Tupperware before you stuck food in your electric fridge. So give Louis a break. It's the FDA's fault for promoting it.

"But it says 'raw' on the packaging!" Well, it's not. It's a lie. The FDA allows the almond companies to still use "raw" in their deceptive labeling—sort of a consolation prize, I guess. Don't care? Well, you should, because the nutrition's being taken out of your food and you don't even know about it. Wake up, man! "But they did it for our health, right?" Not really. More to cover the food companies' own asses after the salmonella-tainted-almond scares of 2001 and 2004. Just thirty-three people were hospitalized. If you think that's bad, check out the tomato's track record.

The raw deal is that, whether or not it's pasteurized, food produced and stored in unsanitary conditions is what actually causes disease. Pasteurization just promotes unclean factories. Other foods that have mandatory pasteurization in the United States: milk, butter, cheese, cream, vinegar, sauerkraut, yogurt, and eggs. When you're filling the shopping cart, look at which labels say "pasteurized" instead of only worrying about the ones that say "organic," because that food trend is stealing thunder from other important issues. Remember, if you buy "organic," it only means it was once covered in shit.

N°079

THE FACTS

Ronald M. Popeil is an American inventor and pitchman for many products sold solely on television. He is the founder of Ronco. If you have ever watched off-hour TV, he was the king of infomercials. He coined the phrases "But wait . . . There's more!", "Now how much would you pay?", and "Set it and forget it!" Some of his inventions include the Chop-o-Matic, the Dial-O-Matic, the Veg-O-Matic, the Pocket Fisherman, the Showtime Rotisserie, and, of course, his reason for making the RIFE list, the GLH Hair System.

Embarrassed by that bald spot? Don't worry, Ron Popeil's hair in a can will fix you in a jiffy. Just match your hair color, give the can a shake, spray, and PRESTO, you will have the look of more hair instantly! You can, once again, have the confidence you deserve for only $9.95! But wait, there's more. Call within then next fifteen minutes and we will double your order and also include a depleted sense of self-worth and the loss of most of your dignity.

[you] RIFE!

Ron didn't ruin it by being a pioneer in selling gimmicky products on TV—hell, he provided us with countless hours of late-night entertainment. Ron ruined it by tempting normal, rational (but apparently desperate) people to believe in sketchy products they see on TV. Even though common sense tells them it won't work, they still think there's a chance it might. History has proven time and again that it's just too easy to believe in something you really want to be true. Thanks, Ron; not only did you destroy self-esteem, you also made people look stupid with dark beads of sweat running down their bald spots.

Other products and techniques for hair loss:

- Hair plugs. Okay, these sort of work, but in the end, you look like a freaky life-size doll.
- The comb-over. Come on, you're not fooling anyone.
- Toupees. Only good if you feel like hatching some robin's eggs.
- Pills and topical agents. They barely work and you need to take them for the rest of your life!
- Hair transplants. This is the only thing that works. They take hair from the back of your head and relocate it to the bald spot. It's expensive and you might have to do it twice.

№080

James Mack Jr.
For adding MORE worry to nursing homes.

THE FACTS

In 2001, James Mack was employed at an old folks' home in Tulsa, Oklahoma. One night, he showed up at work when he was not scheduled to and snuck into a patient's room. Then, instead of walking out the door, he decided to exit through a window—while dragging an eighty-five-year-old female Alzheimer's patient with him. Then Mack proceeded to rape her somewhere outside the building. She was later found lying on the street by an off-duty police officer at 5 AM.

The sleaze, of course, denied the accusation. While medical evidence showed she was indeed raped, he claims she initiated their encounter by grabbing his "little jimmy." Experts agreed that, given her medical condition, the elderly lady was of unsound mind and was not capable of giving consent. And with the help of DNA testing, he was tried and convicted of first-degree granny-rape and sentenced to thirty-five years in prison.

[you] RIFE!

It is a somber decision to relocate an elderly family member to a nursing home. People who do are often riddled with guilt and fear about improper treatment and care for their ailing loved ones. But until Mack, no one feared a hoary medicated molestation. Now, not only do we have to worry about negligent treatment, but we also have to fear that the staff may forcibly ravage our helpless relatives. As if our consciences weren't already giving us an ulcer.

James Mack is the true definition of scumbag. We now have a limitless understanding of just how far a rapist will go. How do people like this sleep at night? Hopefully, in Mack's case, teary-eyed from posterior pain after a hard visit to the prison shower. It's nice when life comes full circle . . . don't you think?

Oh Jimmy Mack, we hope you never come back.

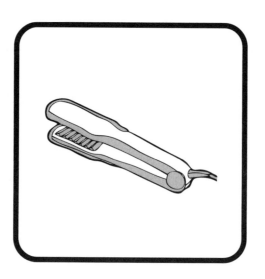

№ 081 | Barbra Streisand
For crimped hair.

THE FACTS

If you are like me and already despise Barbra Streisand, or if you were just waiting for a reason not to like her, then this one's for you . . .

The modern crimping iron was specifically invented for Streisand's hair in 1972 by one of the founders of Sebastian. It was undoubtedly one of the biggest hair mistakes ever conceived. The fear of having to see any additional images of this hairstyle resulted in me *not* finding the designer's intent or inspiration. We can only assume it was to detract from certain facial features. What we do know is that this hideous hairdo, in its time, became hugely popular; the rest is bad-hair history. This fact alone should make you cringe at the sound of Barbra's voice.

What else is wrong with Babs? She always seems to stick that self-righteous beak where it doesn't belong. She is annoying and egotistical, not to mention that she sues anyone for anything. She even sued a California coastline website for having an unmarked aerial photo of her house. Of course she lost and had to pay the defendant's legal fees, hooray! Humorously, these events triggered a new term called "the Streisand effect." It encompasses an attempt to censor information that only results in greater exposure. (This book could always use some added press . . . Go on, Streisand, I dare you!)

[you] RIFE!

Barbra's smug attitude crimps our style. She ruins it whenever she opens her mouth. Go away. In honor of Barb's bad hair, here are a few other bad ideas for the head:

- The mullet. Its ambassador was Billy Ray Cyrus. And just when we thought nothing worse could happen to pop culture, Cyrus spawned Miley.
- The rattail. A less conspicuous variation on the mullet. No, it doesn't look better braided.
- The flattop. If you have one of these, keep it and hope someone thinks you're being ironic.
- Teased bangs. Bangs are debatable. But eighties-style seven-inch Aqua Net–teased bangs, need I say more?

№ 082

Edward Seymour
For inventing aerosol spray paint.

THE FACTS

In the 1940s, the concept of aerosol was already in use by a bug spray from the U.S. Army. Edward Seymour built upon this idea and invented spray paint after a suggestion from his wife. The innovation was ingenious and became immediately popular. His very first color, "aluminum," revolutionized the paint industry.

Unfortunately, like most things, the invention had a serious downside: The propellant, made from chlorofluorocarbons, was adversely affecting the earth's ozone layer. If you are not aware, this protective atmospheric layer is critical to life on this planet because it protects us from the sun's harmful radiation and ultraviolet rays (see RIFE №011).

After it was discovered that CFCs were harmful to the ozone, several nations and organizations worked together to ban the use of the propellant on a global scale.

[you] RIFE!

I know you didn't mean to, Edward, but you put holes in our ozone layer.

If that's not bad enough, you also gave delinquent kids a medium to express their "art" all over buildings and bridges. Prior to the invention of aerosol paint, the prevalence of graffiti was low, since carrying brushes and paint cans was a bit cumbersome. And I won't even get into the "huffing" subculture you instigated.

Whatever happened to our depleting ozone layer anyway? Did it ever re-plete? Will someone please ask Al Gore for me?

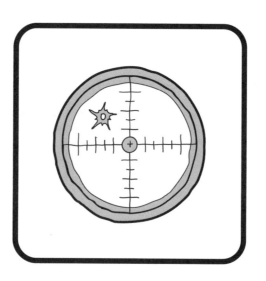

№ 083 | Thomas Hamilton
For causing the handgun ban in the U.K.

THE FACTS

In 1996, Thomas Hamilton went on a killing rampage at Dunblane Primary School with four licensed handguns and seven hundred rounds of ammunition. He committed suicide with a shot in the mouth after murdering sixteen students and one teacher and wounding seventeen others.

Shortly thereafter, the British government banned virtually all handguns from public ownership in hopes of reducing the number of gun-toting freaks. Unfortunately, the plan has surely backfired. The number of gun-related killings and injuries rose more than fourfold since the ban. Whoops! It's been difficult to pinpoint the reason for the surge in gunplay; for simplicity, we'll just blame Guy Ritchie's movies.

[you] RIFE!

As it is written on the T-shirt of 007's nemesis, Jaws, in *Happy Gilmore*, "Guns don't kill people, I kill people." The main problem is that you cannot legislate against mentally disturbed people. The "bad guys" will still get their hands on guns, and the "good guys" will not even have an option to defend themselves with arms. Even if you could keep guns out of the hands of villains (which you can't), villains would just find another murderous tool: a knife, a bomb, an airplane, or a car. Perhaps, you should just have stricter laws about who can purchase a gun. Then you could take advantage of the fact that it's easier to keep tabs on someone when a gun is registered. Just look how well it works in the U.S., where gun violence in schools is virtually nonexistent!

№084

Dean Kamen
For making the future look dorky.

THE FACTS

Dean Kamen invented the Segway in 2001. It's an electric two-wheeled personal transporter. The apparatus uses very precise gyroscopic sensors to keep its balance. The operation of the device is simple—just lean forward to advance, lean back to reverse, and lean the handle bar left or right for either direction. It's quite an extraordinary invention. It practically defies gravity. Unfortunately, when you ride it, it makes you look like a complete dumb-ass.

As the joke goes, "What do mopeds and fat chicks have in common? They're both fun to ride until your friends catch you." Now we can add the Segway to that list for the trifecta.

[you] RIFE!

The thought of what the future might be and look like has interested and perplexed us all. We speculate as to what buildings, cities, cars, computers, fashion, and many other things will look like in the years to come. Usually, our mind conjures up something very cool and original. We see this translated into concept designs, movies, and art. Unfortunately, our perception is always much more sophisticated than the actual usable end products. The Segway is a prime example of this. Gliding along a flat surface without moving our legs is exciting in theory. However, the actual apparatus and the person riding it look lamer than Screech on rollerblades.

Aside from poor aesthetics, the Segway doesn't exactly promote good health, either. In fact, it encourages obesity and laziness. Sure it's fun, but do you need really to glide everywhere? Remember, the more you exercise in life, the better off you will be. So ditch the Segway and start struttin'.

№085

E85
For being a sucky fuel.

THE FACTS

Everyone knows that the U.S. needs to kick its addiction to petroleum. This environmentally harmful, nonrenewable energy comes mainly from foreign countries. We need to push for energy independence, which can only be achieved by using alternative fuels.

E85 is a fuel blended from 85 percent bioethanol and 15 percent gasoline. Many cars have been produced or converted to use this "flex fuel," but its popularity faded after certain statistics were revealed. For example, if we used all the corn produced in the U.S. to make ethanol, we would only displace 3.5 percent of our gasoline demand. This amount of fuel could be compensated just by properly inflating our tires. And it takes gobs of gas just to transport it due to the lack of pipelines in the Midwest.

[you] RIFE!

E85 fooled us. We really wanted it to be the answer to our problems. But we should have known there's no such thing as a quick fix. The reality is that we have to stop using food crops for ethanol. It creates an entirely new kind of stress on the planet by reducing both our food supply and a vital global export. Even if we switched to cheaper non-food crops to produce ethanol, it would still create volatility. If you think gasoline prices are unsteady now, just imagine how a drought would affect the cost of ethanol. And can you really call it an alternative to oil when E85 is only 85 percent ethanol—and 15 percent gasoline? It doesn't sound like much freedom from oil dependency to me. But that opinion may differ if you ask a politician who has his or her hands deep in Big Oil's pockets.

№086^{ed} | General Motors
For killing the electric car.

THE FACTS

The EV1 was an electric vehicle introduced by GM in 1996. The futuristic car was the first modern production electric car available for lease from a major automaker. This zippy vehicle was high-powered, produced zero emissions, and could run for approximately one hundred miles on one charge. Its drivers loved it. Of course, GM did not see it as a moneymaker and decided to destroy all of the vehicles once the leases were up. However, a kindergartener could have told GM to just sell the cars to recoup some lost revenue—instead of pulverizing them in the car crusher. After that, General Motors decided to abandon its electric vehicle technology and put its efforts towards the petrol-pounding Hummer. Hindsight surely mocks them with a resounding DOH! It's speculated that the EV1 program was eliminated because it threatened the excessively powerful oil industry. But who really knows?

[you] RIFE!

Way to go, GM! You had a good thing and you ruined it. You took our only affordable option for an electric car away from us. You ruined it for yourself and everyone else who wanted an alternative to gasoline-gobbling SUVs. Lots of people loved the subcompact and wanted to buy it when their leases were up. However, you 86'd it. Is there any wonder why you had to declare bankruptcy? Next time the wheels in your head start spinning, be certain they are not lug-nutted to a gas guzzler.

As of the year 2009, your latest slaughter tally was around 66,500 jobs lost, 1,100 dealerships closed, and the near-collapse of Detroit. And that's the good news. Try not to forget you still owe 450,000 retirees $90 billion in pensions all while trying to pay back the $27 billion borrowed from the bailout and another $5.7 billion from other governments. We all hope you can pull it together, really. We're excited about the hype for the new electric car, the Volt. But maybe you should call it the Déjà Vu. Hopefully we can actually keep this one . . .

№ 187

Michael John Anderson
For the first Craigslist murder.

THE FACTS

Katherine Ann Olson responded, via e-mail, to an ad on Craigslist in Minnesota for a babysitting job. She accepted the job and showed up expecting to look after the children of a woman named Amy. A day later, her body was found in the trunk of her car, ankles bound with red twine. Her killer was a cold-blooded nineteen-year-old named Michael John Anderson. He lured her into his house and shot her. Police say Anderson killed the twenty-four-year-old woman in his parents' bedroom.

According to Craigslist, this was the first murder involving the widely used online resource for classified advertisements.

[you] RIFE!

Okay, Mr. Creative, ever watch *CSI*? First off, computers are highly traceable. And why couldn't you just have been a normal serial killer? You know, someone who leaves a calling card like bugs in your victims' throats. Or someone who owns an albino pet. Besides, you should've waited until you were highly educated and entirely off the grid before you got caught. You could've toyed with the cops by burning off your fingerprints and FedEx-ing severed heads to the desert. Or you could've just stapled an I DID IT note to your forehead while lying on your victim's trunk. But maybe that would've made it harder for the police to find you . . .

I guess it was inevitable that someone would eventually die as a result of our beloved Craigslist. But it still makes me shake my head in denial. So we must blame Anderson for leaving us wondering if we'll be the next victim. Now we are scared even when we want to sell an old stained couch online to a couple of college freshmen! I still wonder if it was a contract killing. I smell a conspiracy here. Did eBay hire you? Someone get its marketing department on the phone . . .

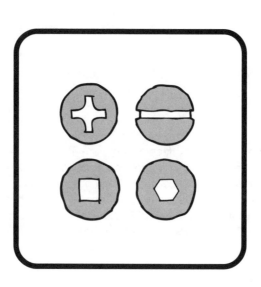

№088

THE FACTS

Phillips, slotted, square, or Allen. Just pick one, for Christ's sake!

In 1908, square-drive screws were invented by Canadian P.L. Robertson. This was the first recess-drive-type fastener for production usage. The previous single-slotted head allowed for too much tool slippage.

Then, in 1933, the Phillips-head screw was invented by Henry Phillips. Automobile manufacturers were now using assembly lines. They needed screws that could take a lot of torque but could also slip out (or cam out) to prevent overtightening. The Phillips design solved this problem.

From there on, everybody and their little sisters invented a new type of screw head just because Phillips started the trend. Here are a few: Torx, tri-wing, torq-set, triple square, spanner head, spline drive, double hex, polydrive, clutch, and Bristol.

[you] RIFE!

Phillips, you're a tool. We were doing just fine with the square one. Did we really need another type of screw head? I don't buy that automotive "slip out" theory. Perhaps Sears hired you so they could sell more tools? Whatever your reasons were, to this day, no matter what type of screw needs tightening, we will always have the wrong type of screwdriver in hand.

And please, if you are a company manufacturing something that comes unassembled and includes or requires a "special tool" to construct it, STOP the madness. We don't need any more crappy tools we can easily lose. Yes, we are talking to you, IKEA!

№089

Tian Wenhua
For poisoning milk.

THE FACTS

Melamine is used in making many industrial products. It can be found in countertops, fabrics, glue, Formica, cleaning products, and pesticides. It is, however, quite dangerous and even deadly if ingested. Not exactly something you would want to pour into your morning coffee.

Tian Wenhua was chairwoman and general manager of the Sanlu Group, one of China's largest dairy companies. She is responsible for adding melamine to the company's milk in order to spike the protein levels for quality control testing. As a result of Wenhua's decision, at least six infants would die and three hundred thousand others would suffer from kidney stones and other urinary problems. She is now serving a life sentence in jail for her role in the tainted-milk scandal.

Hundreds of edible products were affected around the world, including powdered baby milk, cookies, candy, chocolate, ice cream, and more.

[you] RIFE!

FYI—the amount of pesticide that should be in your 2 percent is 0 percent! Tian's recklessness and blatant disregard for human health and well-being is difficult to fathom. What could have driven the milky judgments that lead her to believe this was acceptable? It's one thing to profit from stealing, but quite another to profit from poisoning people.

You can't help but wonder what drinks she avoids in the slammer—we'll just assume she's lactose-intolerant.

Walter Diemer
For making a sticky mess of things.

THE FACTS

In 1869, William Finley Semple became the first person to patent chewing gum. The first attempt at bubble gum was made by Frank Henry Fleer, in 1906. He called it Blibber-Blubber. Fleer's recipe was later perfected by Walter Diemer in 1928, who called his product Double Bubble. This gooey pink concoction changed regular ol' boring chewing gum into the lip-smacking good time of blowin' bubbles. Until, of course, the flavor wears out . . .

[you] RIFE!

We have Mr. Diemer to blow the whistle on every time we step in this gluey goop. No, he did not invent gum, but it's his fault it gained popularity and that things started getting messy.

Now don't get me wrong, I enjoy a stick or two of gum now and again. In fact, I chewed it almost every day as a child (just ask my dentist). The problem is that used gum never seems to find a trash can. Why throw it away properly when you can stick it to something and ruin another person's day? Seriously, show me one person who has never stepped in gum and I will show you a levitating man. It's on the streets and the sidewalks, in parks and under desks and on benches, ready to get on your shoe, in your hair, and on your clothes. It seems like the only place it's not is in the garbage. It's out to get you (or at least on you).

So go ahead if you must, chomp away. But if you do chew gum, when you are through with it, make sure it ends up in the land of tin cans and fish bones. You may also swallow it or stick it behind your ear for disposal. Don't worry: It takes about seven years less than you think to digest. And for Christ's sake, chew it with your mouth closed.

№091 | The United States
For abusing the world's natural resources.

THE FACTS

It's alarming how quickly human beings are burning through the world's natural resources. And although it accounts for only 5 percent of the world's population, the U.S. consumes 26 percent of the world's energy.

And while I'm at it, shame on you too, Canada—per capita you use more energy than anyone!

As far as Italy is concerned, someone go tell Tony and Bruno they can rub it in all of our faces, because, proportionately, "the boot" consumes the least of all. Way to go, Italia!

[you] RIFE!

America, *stop* being so American. It just makes you look ignorant, arrogant, and gluttonous. Realize that your carbon footprint and your existence will have a potentially devastating effect on future generations. Take a step, change something in your life, and make the world a better place.

Top five ways to go green in under five minutes:

1. Bring your own bag to the market.
2. Unplug things that stay on for no reason.
3. Do full loads of laundry, not many small ones.
4. Take short showers, not baths.
5. Adjust your thermostat up one degree in the summer and down one degree in the winter.

Now was that so hard?

№092

The New York Mercantile Exchange
For driving up the price of gas.

THE FACTS

Okay, okay, I know I said gas was bad and we should find alternative fuels, etc., etc. But let's be realistic—it ain't happening anytime soon. So it's time to dip into the problem . . . The New York Mercantile Exchange is the world's largest commodity futures exchange. This is where energy products and other commodities are bought and sold. Oil is among the most heavily traded. Exxon Mobil reported $45.2 billion in profits for 2008. That's right, $45.2 B-I-L-L-I-O-N in one year. That is $150 for every man, woman, and child in the U.S. How is this possible? I give you the New York Mercantile Exchange to blame. And why? Money, duh!

[you] RIFE!

Maybe I'm missing something here, but it seems to me that the price of gas should be determined by how much it costs to pull the oil from the ground and then refine, transport, and distribute it, plus tax. That should be it, right? Unfortunately, it's not. Buying and selling oil on speculation at the New York Mercantile Exchange (and London's ICE Futures) is to blame for the capricious pricing. It has nothing to do with myths of "peak oil" or supply and demand. The process of trading "paper oil" is very opaque. Actually understanding the "who" and "why" is about as transparent as West Texas crude.

We can all agree that gas prices are out of whack and about as stable as Britney's mental health. The lack of regulation has only enhanced the confusion and greed. The NYME needs a babysitter, that's all there is to it. We have already learned that we can't trust greedy businessmen with power. As my high school world history teacher frequently reminded us, "Power corrupts, and absolute power corrupts *absolutely*."

№093

The paparazzi
For causing the death of a princess.

THE FACTS

Except for Twitter, who cares what Britney ate for breakfast? Not us. Nor do we care what Nicole puked up. And please, TMZ, only report Lindsay's car accidents that the tabloids don't cause. Here's an eye-opener: I'll bet you heard plenty on Paris's trip to the slammer. But did you know Kiefer Sutherland served forty-eight days behind bars a couple years ago? If you did, give yourself a gold star. But for the rest of us, I guess he's just too old, doesn't have boobs, and hasn't starred in enough leaked porn videos for us to care.

Saying the paparazzi have gone too far would be like saying Chris Brown only gave Rihanna a light love tap. And by this point, we're bored with it. All of it. I know it's hard to feel sorry for some celebs with all that money and fame and such. And you'd probably want to spit on them if you knew their real personalities anyway. But—you don't. The only personality you know is what's hyped in the tabloids. That'd be cool if the gossip were true. Because sleeping in an oxygen chamber sounds like fun to me (if for no other reason than to escape the paparazzi). And sure, if it was good enough for Walt, I also want to be cryogenically frozen when I die! And if Mikey died doing it, then I won't eat Pop Rocks and drink soda either!

But what's worse is that the paparazzi not only fabricate ridiculous rumors, but they also drive these poor celebrities off the edge. No wonder Britney shaved her head . . . I would've too! Which brings us to the reason for this entry: The paparazzi, in their endless quest for the next headliner, helped killed Princess Diana. Remember? Her car swerved head-on into a pillar inside a tunnel going 65 mph while being chased by the photographers. In 2008, a jury determined that the driver, Henri Paul, and the *paparazzi* were to blame. Guilty of gross negligent (princess) slaughter.

[you] RIFE!

You destroy lives *and* you killed a princess. That's wrong on so many levels. Just so you know, it's impossible for a car chase to exist if there's no one pursuing (just ask O.J.). Where are your scruples? Stop being a glorified peeping Tom and ease off. Get a life and try not to destroy one. Quit your day job. If you still want people to hate you, join Greenpeace. And if you still want to work for a non-reputable news source, send your résumé to Fox News.

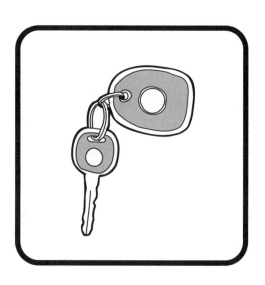

№094

Los Angeles
For promoting valet parking.

THE FACTS

Valet parking is described in the dictionary as a service offered by a hotel, restaurant, etc., through which patrons' cars are parked by an attendant. Perhaps you've never seen this service? You either don't have a car or never dine out. Either way, if you have not experienced one, you might be labeled a cheap bastard.

[you] RIFE!

Los Angeles started promoting this senseless status symbol in the 1940s. I guess the Hollywood elite felt comfortable driving their own cars, but self-parking was just SO 1930s. Whatever the reason, the tradition somehow stuck, and now we have to pay a minimum of $4.50 at many ordinary restaurants and hotels to be, usually, inconvenienced. Seriously, it doesn't make me feel any more upper class to have my car parked for me at the Cheesecake Factory.

Don't get me wrong—there are a few good reasons to valet park. Perhaps there is no other parking available, or it may take longer than fifteen minutes to walk from a self-found parking space, or maybe the weather is bad. In these cases, it's worth it, and I am all for it! However, many establishments around the country feel they must have mandatory valet parking even though there are huge, nearly empty dedicated parking lots adjacent to the restaurants. This is about as useful as a screen door on a submarine.

What if they skipped the parking part and just cleaned your car, or added some windshield washer fluid, or replaced the breaks, or gave you an alignment? I wouldn't feel ripped-off if they did that. But no, instead, they just lollygag to your car and bring it back to you in the same or worse condition in which you gave it to them.

Here are the new RIFE laws: Twenty seconds or less or it's free. If you can physically see your car from the valet stand, then it's free. If it takes longer to wait for some guy to get the car than it would to walk to it, it's free. If they don't run to your car, it's free. If they stink up the car, it's probably from the BO caused from running, but it will still be free. I don't like your cheesecake anyway.

№095

MTV
For making "reality TV" a reality.

THE FACTS

MTV (in case you've been on a constant Xanax drip since birth) stands for Music Television. MTV had a good thing going with music videos, music news, band interviews, and, in general, shows about—you guessed it—music! So what makes a music TV station put non-music-related reality shows on the air? Brain damage. Every boob tube junkie's grasp on "reality" was forever changed with the airing of a show called *The Real World*.

What gets pumped through the idiot box has radically changed since the birth of television. The years have morphed ten channels of simple black-and-white telecasting into plasma simulcasting in HD via satellite. TV used to be my buddy. As a kid I could cuddle up to *Mr. Rogers*, *Sesame Street*, and *The Smurfs*. As I grew up, so did my shows: *The Simpsons*, *Friends,* and *Seinfeld*. But somewhere along the line, reality TV ratings began to soar. We traded in our *Family Ties* for "real" lives. We swapped our *Cheers* for realistic tears. Shows like *The Bachelor*, *American Idol*, *Survivor*, and *Fear Factor* began to dominate prime time. Scripted TV went down faster than Jack Bauer could chug a beer.

[you] RIFE!

I hold MTV responsible. Yeah, there were other reality television shows before, but none that left its audience violently drooling like a crack addict waiting for a visual fix, and none that rotted as many brain cells.

Let's face it, reality TV is just a way for producers to save a buck by cutting out the middleman in television production—you know, the actors and writers. However, the reality becomes blurred when you realize that these shows are usually scripted, doctored, over-edited, over-shot, and reshot. Unfortunately, this "reality" is about as honest as Tony Soprano's waste management company.

It wouldn't be so bad if it were quality programming, but who really wants to see eight three-foot-tall circus midgets competing for the Octomom's hand in marriage? . . . Wait a minute, that might be good . . . I hope I TiVo'd that!

Charles Darwin
For proving God wrong.

THE FACTS

Charles Darwin was born in 1809. He was a British naturalist who became famous for his theory of evolution and natural selection. He believed that all life on earth evolved over millions of years from a few common ancestors. He was not the first to have these beliefs, but he was undoubtedly the most famous to bring them to light. His theory of evolutionary selection reveals that variations within species occur randomly and the survival or extinction of each organism is determined by that organism's ability to survive, adapt, and reproduce in its environment.

On a side note, Darwin's father almost saved him from ruining it for everyone. His dad nearly prohibited the devout doubter from going on his science expedition in 1831. He was scared it would lead him away from a future in the clergy. Oops! I hope he went to confession after that one.

[you] RIFE!

Holy shit, Chuck! You made us doubt our divine maker. Your theories are in direct conflict with the church and the Bible. And now, ever since this crazy hypothesis, "science" and "religion" can't play nicely together.

Don't worry, religion. Evolution is just a theory. It will most likely be forgotten in a few hundred years anyway. It's not proven, like the Bible is. And it's not based on something as concrete as faith! Besides, what more does science have to offer than watching miniature volcanoes explode at the science fair?

Don't worry, science. Religion may still go out of style. I mean, the two largest religions are less than two thousand years old (Islam originated in 610 AD and Christianity in 30 AD). If you are worried, you should start a support group where you can study and read passages from text-books together. You can meet once a week in your spare time, maybe on Sunday mornings? And even if you're wrong, I am sure you've got equipment that can measure just how hot hell might be.

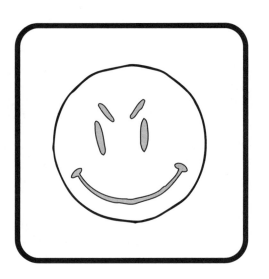

Wal-Mart shoppers
For buying a gallon of pickles for $2.97.

THE FACTS

The only two Dow Jones stocks to rise in 2008 were Wal-Mart, with an 18 percent gain, and McDonald's, at 6 percent. Wal-Mart sells more than Target, Sears, Kmart, JC Penney, Safeway, and Kroger combined.

What's wrong with Wal-Mart? Nothing, legally. For the most part, it's legit. We have to blame capitalism and the consumer for its repugnant reign.

[you] RIFE!

Wal-Mart does everything it can to get its shoppers that low, low price. The Vlasic Pickle Company quickly discovered the power of the giant superstore. Wal-Mart wanted to make a statement for its low prices by selling a gallon jar of pickles for $2.97. Vlasic went along with the idea and the enormous jar sold like crazy. Every store was selling about eighty jars a week. That's nearly a million gallons of pickles a month. Wal-Mart sure put Vlasic in a pickle with the experiment. It did dramatically increase the pickle company's sales, but drastically reduced its profits, lowered the company's image, and adversely affected farmers. Wal-Mart also ruined it for Master Lock and Levi's in similar ways.

Yes, Wal-Mart is the devil. It's widely known that it has poor employment strategies, forces local businesses into bankruptcy, squeezes suppliers, promotes overseas manufacturing, destroys nature, and sucks government assistance dry. But who cares? Obviously not consumers. They already know that Wal-Mart is sketchy, yet they shop there anyway. And the government is not going to step in since the company plays by the rules. If you don't like it, don't shop there. What would you do with a gallon jar of pickles anyway?

№098

Pamela and Gela of Juicy Couture
For making the velour tracksuit popular.

THE FACTS

Pamela Skaist-Levy and Gela Nash-Taylor founded Juicy Couture, a clothing company, in 1994. They started their tracksuit line in 1999. The outfit was an older idea that Juicy decided to make sassy by slapping its logo on the ass and selling it at a really high price point. Pamela and Gela had a smart marketing ploy: They let top celebrities like Madonna shop their line for free. Then the celebs were photographed wearing Juicy Couture's clothing. After that, the brand and outfit became a smash hit.

Okay, so Juicy Couture did not start bad fashion; it just happened to create one of the worst fashion trends. If you own this ensemble, don't throw it away (unless you're a man). You can wear the top or the bottom; just try to refrain from wearing them at the same time. Think about it—have you ever been asked out while wearing this outfit? If so, I am sure the relationship ended with a restraining order.

[you] RIFE!

There has been bad fashion since we stopped walking around naked. Is it Juicy's fault? Is it the designers' fault for creating bad fashion? Or is it the consumers' fault for buying it? Or should we blame Madonna for wearing free shit? Here are some other horrifying fashion faux pas:

- Shoulder pads. (Because looking like a linebacker is just so feminine.)
- Leg warmers. (Thanks a lot, *Flashdance*!)
- Pants fallin' off the ass. (It could be worse—men could go back to showing off their bulges.)
- High-waisted "mom" jeans. (Great idea—wear something that makes your ass look bigger!)
- Uggs. (Nothing says fashion like puffy arctic boots in the summertime.)
- Socks with flip-flops. (This was never a trend; it was just stupid. If God wanted you to wear this, he would have made socks like mittens, but he didn't, so stop doing it.)
- Popped collars. (Ever notice that the preppy douche bag in the movies always has his collar up? Think about it. Even if the style comes back, just say NO.)

THE FACTS

In case you are not from Canada, curling is an Olympic "sport." It involves pushing a granite stone on ice and then sweeping brooms in front of it. It takes a tremendous amount of skill and precision. If you wanna play, get some friends together in the wintertime. Grab a push broom, steal a few big flat stones from the neighbor's yard, and head for the frozen creek. Then take the stones and throw them at your friends' kneecaps. After that, proceed to beat the shit out of them with the broom for agreeing to play such a stupid game.

Curling is what people did for fun in Scotland in the sixteenth century . . . Some traditions should just die. I mean, seriously, we let you keep the kilt and bagpipe. The only reason you are not the world's worst country ever is because you invented Scotch and you're the birth place of the best James Bond. (No, not Timothy Dalton.)

[you] RIFE!

Curling is basically shuffleboard on ice (that thing that old people play in Florida). If Tampa ever gets to host the Winter Olympics, Grandpa Joe will be a U.S. Olympic hopeful.

Other bad Olympic sports that desperately need eradication:

- Shooting. This is great exercise for ONE eyelid. You don't break a sweat or have your heart rise above 48 bpm. If you want respect, do the biathlon instead (skiing AND rifle shooting).
- Synchronized swimming. Actually, this takes lots of skill, but nobody cares to watch a few athletes splashing each other while clothed. If you want better ratings, add chicken fights!
- Race walking. Someone check the rule book—I don't think oxymorons are even allowed . . .
- Table tennis. We can keep this if they start allowing air hockey and foosball! If not, then let's yank it from the roster. (But wait till after Biba Golic retires.)
- Diving. Even gays think it's gay.
- Trampoline. It's better than diving. But it's a trampoline. It's a backyard activity for children. If we keep this, then we should allow badminton and beach volleyball too—oh, wait . . .
- Equestrian sports. Okay—then do I get to ride on my luck dragon in the 100-meter dash?

№ 100

Shawn Meneely
For eliminating diving boards.

THE FACTS

Imagine, if you will, it is summertime and a fourteen-year-old boy is having a blast at the neighbor's pool. He and his friends are taking turns jumping off the diving board. The enthusiastic teenager springs off the board and attempts a suicide dive (a suicide dive involves jumping off a board headfirst with your arms at your sides). Quickly after entering the water, his head smashes into the upslope of the pool and he becomes paralyzed for life. This is the tragedy that happened to Shawn Meneely. His parents were crushed and angrily sued the National Spa & Pool Institute, the diving-board manufacturer, and even the pool builder. Shawn won $6.6 million from the NSPI. Now, thanks to the Meneelys and their lawyers, all backyard-pool diving boards have felt the sting of a painful belly flop.

The National Spinal Cord Injury Statistical Center reports that eight hundred Americans are permanently paralyzed as a result of diving accidents every year. More impressively, about three thousand people drown yearly without any help from diving boards. (Maybe it's time to outlaw pools too.)

[you] RIFE!

The gainer, jackknife, swan dive, flip, and, of course, the CANNONBALL! Everyone got wet when you did that. Those were the days. Your summers were set if you had a friend with a pool and a board. Now diving boards have nearly vanished because of one clumsy boy and his greedy lawyers. I am all for safety and security, but there is a limit and it has gotten ridiculous. STOP taking the fun out of everything! Shit happens regardless. We don't live in a white-padded-wall world, although with crazy lawsuits like these diving at our sanity, we may all end up there.

Afterward, Mr. Meneely tried to become an advocate for diving board safety—but really, he just became the poster boy for its eradication. So you still want a diving board? Well, too bad, because you need proper pool sizing. I know what you're thinking—you will just have a pool built to the proper distance and depth. Well, it turns out, if you build it, they WON'T come. No insurance company will underwrite a diving board. And it doesn't matter, because builders won't install one. Thanks for the memories!

№ 101 | **The apple**
For making sin so tasty.

THE FACTS

Here's the story: God was bored and needed some company. So he grabbed some clay and made Adam. God then created a garden for Adam to live in, called Eden. After that he created some cool animals for Adam to hang with. However, God felt a bit guilty because Adam had no one to mack on. So God decided to play matchmaker, grabbed a rib, and made Eve. Then he laid down the ground rules . . . The first rule of Eden: You do not eat from the Tree of Good and Evil. The second rule of Eden: You DO NOT eat from the Tree of Good and Evil! But they ate from it anyway. As a result, God kicked them out and cursed women to forever have horrible pain during childbirth.

Then God felt guilty again, so he created the epidural.

[you] RIFE!

Why did the pesky apple have to be so enticing in the first place? Now all of humankind is a bunch of no-good sinners all because of some mouthwatering Golden Delicious. But let's be realistic, it had some help . . .

Way to go, Eve. You listened to some stupid talking snake and took the first bite of the apple. And then you tempted Adam with it. So step up and take some blame, sister.

Way to go, Adam. It's more your fault for being a dope. You ate the apple just for a cute piece of ass. WAKE UP, man! You had the perfect "desert island" scenario. She would have totally let you bone her no matter what! Nice going, loser.

Way to go, God. You put the tempting tree there to begin with. And why put limits on the couple? What are you, some kind of control freak? And why are we, to this day, still paying for someone else's mistake? And if you really think about it, it's your fault for not making us perfect in the first place!

So if [you] made it in this book—or even if you ruined it for just one person—you can still dodge the RIFE finger by pointing the blame back to the preeminently divine ruiner. Thank God!

JOIN THE DISCUSSION

Perhaps you are blaming me for not adding your favorite RIFE. Well, that's because I don't know you. If you like, write me and say, "Matt, You Ruined It For Everyone because you forgot to add [insert person here] to the list!", and then proceed to tell me some funny anecdote as to why. Maybe, if it's not hate mail or a death threat (and it doesn't suck), I will include it in the sequel (you will be credited, of course; however, you will not be remunerated). Email me at matt@youruinedit.com. Or go to the website:

youruinedit.com

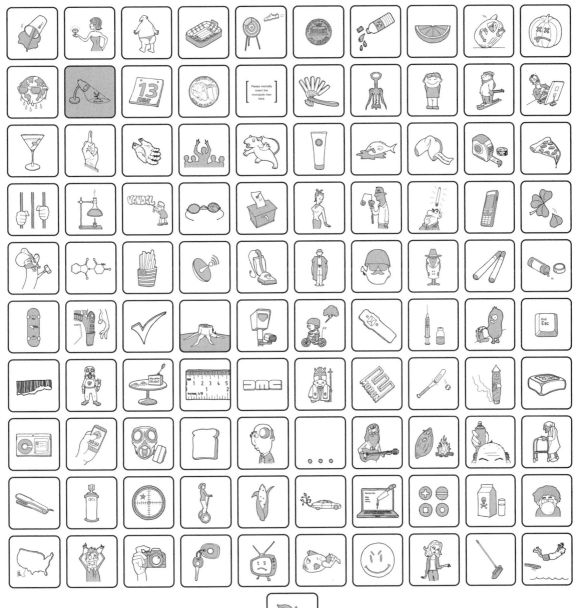

THANK [you] FOR HELPING ME RUIN IT

Thanks to all the RIFErs who made this book possible! Your misjudgment, neglect and ignorance give us all a reason to grumble. Best wishes!

Support:
[Mélanie R.] For all of your support and for being my favorite person.
[Téa V.] For being my main inspiration to expose and rid the world of all ruiners!
[Lucy C.] This book would be nothing without you, plain and simple. Thank you.
[Denise O.] For believing in me, making me smarter, and putting this book on the shelves.
[David V.] For being the best dad and best editor before I had an editor.
[Tony N.] For making me aware that it takes six times to see dead people.
[Pat V.] For being the best mom and always supporting my dreams.
[Julie V.] For the great RIFE ideas and the excellent inspiration.
[Brian V.] For thinking everything is a conspiracy.
[Chris V.] For thinking nothing is a conspiracy.
[Gavin V.] For questioning the conspiracy.
[Louise R.] For always laughing.
[Richard R.] For always pointing the finger (even though it's usually the wrong one).
[Tony P.] For helping me understand the industry.
[Keith G. + Monique G.] For all of your support.
[Christian L.] For the author-to-author advice and pep talk.

Prereaders:
[Neal F. + Crystal F.] For being my best Indiana friends.
[Kevin K.] For being my best New York friend.
[Scott S. + Melodie S.] For being my best Los Angeles friends.
[Grant K. + Shea K. family] For letting your kids read it!
[Max M. + Melissa M.] Max, maybe you didn't read it, but I felt the support.
[Alex V.] For being tough, honest, and great.
[Scott R.] For not getting bored.
[Steve S.] For always being a great guy and wearing the T-shirt!
[Alexis R.] For being my liaison to Tony, and for sneaking a read and liking it.
[Tanya B.] For being my interested local bookstore employee.
[Carole M.] For being a great second set of eyes.

Educators:
[Wes J.] For being my most influential architecture prof.
[Laura S.] For being my most influential English prof.

Resources:
[Google] For being the best search engine.
[Dictionary.com] For being the best free resource.
[iStockphoto.com] For being royalty-free.

Permissions:
Actually, I only got one permission, but I decided not to use it.
Here's some free advertising for the companies that said NO:
[Rhino Records] For NOT letting me use the Grateful Dead logo, Steal Your Face, on RIFE Nº077.
[Craigslist.org] Craig's great but indecisive, I'm still waiting on a response to use their logo on RIFE NºO87.
[UPMC] For NOT letting me use a can of Spam on RIFE Nº063.
[Hasbro] For nothing, see RIFE Nº015.

RATE IT!

How badly did they ruin it for you?
Keep track and share it online!

youruinedit.com

[you] rife

SCORECARD

FUBAR	badly	so-so	barely		
[ ]	[ ]	[ ]	[ ]	001	Stella Liebeck
[ ]	[ ]	[ ]	[ ]	002	De Beers
[ ]	[ ]	[ ]	[ ]	003	Peter Travis
[ ]	[ ]	[ ]	[ ]	004	Anheuser-Busch
[ ]	[ ]	[ ]	[ ]	005	Muntadhar al-Zeidi
[ ]	[ ]	[ ]	[ ]	006	The U.S. Treasury and Mint
[ ]	[ ]	[ ]	[ ]	007	Abdulla Ahmed Ali
[ ]	[ ]	[ ]	[ ]	008	Tropicana
[ ]	[ ]	[ ]	[ ]	009	Gordon Dancy
[ ]	[ ]	[ ]	[ ]	010	Ronald Clark O'Bryan
[ ]	[ ]	[ ]	[ ]	011	Al Gore
[ ]	[ ]	[ ]	[ ]	012	George Vernon Hudson
[ ]	[ ]	[ ]	[ ]	013	Triskaidekaphobia (fearing the number 13)
[ ]	[ ]	[ ]	[ ]	014	Thomas Jefferson
[ ]	[ ]	[ ]	[ ]	015	Ticketmaster
[ ]	[ ]	[ ]	[ ]	016	Gillette
[ ]	[ ]	[ ]	[ ]	017	Robert Ramon
[ ]	[ ]	[ ]	[ ]	018	Mary Kay Letourneau
[ ]	[ ]	[ ]	[ ]	019	Sonny Bono and Michael Kennedy
[ ]	[ ]	[ ]	[ ]	020	McGraw-Hill
[ ]	[ ]	[ ]	[ ]	021	Alcohol
[ ]	[ ]	[ ]	[ ]	022	The inventor of plastic packaging
[ ]	[ ]	[ ]	[ ]	023	O.J. Simpson's (first) jury
[ ]	[ ]	[ ]	[ ]	024	Guy standing up at a concert
[ ]	[ ]	[ ]	[ ]	025	Richard Gere
[ ]	[ ]	[ ]	[ ]	026	Coppertone
[ ]	[ ]	[ ]	[ ]	027	BP
[ ]	[ ]	[ ]	[ ]	028	Chinese boys
[ ]	[ ]	[ ]	[ ]	029	Dick Fuld
[ ]	[ ]	[ ]	[ ]	030	Thomas Monaghan
[ ]	[ ]	[ ]	[ ]	031	Guantánamo Bay
[ ]	[ ]	[ ]	[ ]	032	Tweekers
[ ]	[ ]	[ ]	[ ]	033	Chaka
[ ]	[ ]	[ ]	[ ]	034	Mark David Chapman
[ ]	[ ]	[ ]	[ ]	035	Katherine Harris
[ ]	[ ]	[ ]	[ ]	036	Ruth Handler
[ ]	[ ]	[ ]	[ ]	037	Tiger
[ ]	[ ]	[ ]	[ ]	038	Peter Cooper Hewitt
[ ]	[ ]	[ ]	[ ]	039	Dr. Martin Cooper
[ ]	[ ]	[ ]	[ ]	040	Edward A. Murphy
[ ]	[ ]	[ ]	[ ]	041	Clarence Thomas
[ ]	[ ]	[ ]	[ ]	042	Chemie Grünenthal
[ ]	[ ]	[ ]	[ ]	043	W.
[ ]	[ ]	[ ]	[ ]	044	Barack Obama
[ ]	[ ]	[ ]	[ ]	045	Albert and Joe Cobble
[ ]	[ ]	[ ]	[ ]	046	Dr. Seymour Butts
[ ]	[ ]	[ ]	[ ]	047	William Harley and Arthur Davidson
[ ]	[ ]	[ ]	[ ]	048	Insurance frauds
[ ]	[ ]	[ ]	[ ]	049	Big Tobacco
[ ]	[ ]	[ ]	[ ]	050	The Consumer Product Safety Commission
[ ]	[ ]	[ ]	[ ]	051	Michael J. Fox

SCORECARD

FUBAR	badly	so-so	barely		
[ ]	[ ]	[ ]	[ ]	052	Mike Ramsay and Jim Barton
[ ]	[ ]	[ ]	[ ]	053	IBM
[ ]	[ ]	[ ]	[ ]	054	The Yellow Pages
[ ]	[ ]	[ ]	[ ]	055	Maurice Gatsonides
[ ]	[ ]	[ ]	[ ]	056	Overprotective parents
[ ]	[ ]	[ ]	[ ]	057	Jack Welch
[ ]	[ ]	[ ]	[ ]	058	Alex Rodriguez
[ ]	[ ]	[ ]	[ ]	059	The automatic-flush toilet inventor
[ ]	[ ]	[ ]	[ ]	060	Photoshop
[ ]	[ ]	[ ]	[ ]	061	R. Stanton Avery
[ ]	[ ]	[ ]	[ ]	062	Germaphobes
[ ]	[ ]	[ ]	[ ]	063	The U.S. Department of Agriculture
[ ]	[ ]	[ ]	[ ]	064	The imperial system of measurement
[ ]	[ ]	[ ]	[ ]	065	John DeLorean
[ ]	[ ]	[ ]	[ ]	066	Pope Siricius
[ ]	[ ]	[ ]	[ ]	067	Ken Lay and Jeff Skilling
[ ]	[ ]	[ ]	[ ]	068	Scott Boras and Drew Rosenhaus
[ ]	[ ]	[ ]	[ ]	069	Monica Lewinsky
[ ]	[ ]	[ ]	[ ]	070	Tyler Durden
[ ]	[ ]	[ ]	[ ]	071	Sony's Betamax
[ ]	[ ]	[ ]	[ ]	072	Car alarm users
[ ]	[ ]	[ ]	[ ]	073	Asbestos companies
[ ]	[ ]	[ ]	[ ]	074	Dr. Robert Atkins
[ ]	[ ]	[ ]	[ ]	075	Phil Gramm
[ ]	[ ]	[ ]	[ ]	076	*MLA Handbook*
[ ]	[ ]	[ ]	[ ]	077	Blue Star LSD warnings
[ ]	[ ]	[ ]	[ ]	078	The Food and Drug Administration
[ ]	[ ]	[ ]	[ ]	079	Ron Popeil
[ ]	[ ]	[ ]	[ ]	080	James Mack Jr.
[ ]	[ ]	[ ]	[ ]	081	Barbra Streisand
[ ]	[ ]	[ ]	[ ]	082	Edward Seymour
[ ]	[ ]	[ ]	[ ]	083	Thomas Hamilton
[ ]	[ ]	[ ]	[ ]	084	Dean Kamen
[ ]	[ ]	[ ]	[ ]	085	E85
[ ]	[ ]	[ ]	[ ]	086	General Motors
[ ]	[ ]	[ ]	[ ]	087	Michael John Anderson
[ ]	[ ]	[ ]	[ ]	088	Henry Phillips
[ ]	[ ]	[ ]	[ ]	089	Tian Wenhua
[ ]	[ ]	[ ]	[ ]	090	Walter Diemer
[ ]	[ ]	[ ]	[ ]	091	The United States
[ ]	[ ]	[ ]	[ ]	092	The New York Mercantile Exchange
[ ]	[ ]	[ ]	[ ]	093	The paparazzi
[ ]	[ ]	[ ]	[ ]	094	Los Angeles
[ ]	[ ]	[ ]	[ ]	095	MTV
[ ]	[ ]	[ ]	[ ]	096	Charles Darwin
[ ]	[ ]	[ ]	[ ]	097	Wal-Mart shoppers
[ ]	[ ]	[ ]	[ ]	098	Pamela and Gela of Juicy Couture
[ ]	[ ]	[ ]	[ ]	099	Scotland
[ ]	[ ]	[ ]	[ ]	100	Shawn Meneely
[ ]	[ ]	[ ]	[ ]	101	The apple

[you] RiFe

SCORECARD

FUBAR	badly	so-so	barely		
[]	[]	[]	[]	001	Stella Liebeck
[]	[]	[]	[]	002	De Beers
[]	[]	[]	[]	003	Peter Travis
[]	[]	[]	[]	004	Anheuser-Busch
[]	[]	[]	[]	005	Muntadhar al-Zeidi
[]	[]	[]	[]	006	The U.S. Treasury and Mint
[]	[]	[]	[]	007	Abdulla Ahmed Ali
[]	[]	[]	[]	008	Tropicana
[]	[]	[]	[]	009	Gordon Dancy
[]	[]	[]	[]	010	Ronald Clark O'Bryan
[]	[]	[]	[]	011	Al Gore
[]	[]	[]	[]	012	George Vernon Hudson
[]	[]	[]	[]	013	Triskaidekaphobia (fearing the number 13)
[]	[]	[]	[]	014	Thomas Jefferson
[]	[]	[]	[]	015	Ticketmaster
[]	[]	[]	[]	016	Gillette
[]	[]	[]	[]	017	Robert Ramon
[]	[]	[]	[]	018	Mary Kay Letourneau
[]	[]	[]	[]	019	Sonny Bono and Michael Kennedy
[]	[]	[]	[]	020	McGraw-Hill
[]	[]	[]	[]	021	Alcohol
[]	[]	[]	[]	022	The inventor of plastic packaging
[]	[]	[]	[]	023	O.J. Simpson's (first) jury
[]	[]	[]	[]	024	Guy standing up at a concert
[]	[]	[]	[]	025	Richard Gere
[]	[]	[]	[]	026	Coppertone
[]	[]	[]	[]	027	BP
[]	[]	[]	[]	028	Chinese boys
[]	[]	[]	[]	029	Dick Fuld
[]	[]	[]	[]	030	Thomas Monaghan
[]	[]	[]	[]	031	Guantánamo Bay
[]	[]	[]	[]	032	Tweekers
[]	[]	[]	[]	033	Chaka
[]	[]	[]	[]	034	Mark David Chapman
[]	[]	[]	[]	035	Katherine Harris
[]	[]	[]	[]	036	Ruth Handler
[]	[]	[]	[]	037	Tiger
[]	[]	[]	[]	038	Peter Cooper Hewitt
[]	[]	[]	[]	039	Dr. Martin Cooper
[]	[]	[]	[]	040	Edward A. Murphy
[]	[]	[]	[]	041	Clarence Thomas
[]	[]	[]	[]	042	Chemie Grünenthal
[]	[]	[]	[]	043	W.
[]	[]	[]	[]	044	Barack Obama
[]	[]	[]	[]	045	Albert and Joe Cobble
[]	[]	[]	[]	046	Dr. Seymour Butts
[]	[]	[]	[]	047	William Harley and Arthur Davidson
[]	[]	[]	[]	048	Insurance frauds
[]	[]	[]	[]	049	Big Tobacco
[]	[]	[]	[]	050	The Consumer Product Safety Commission
[]	[]	[]	[]	051	Michael J. Fox

SCORECARD

FUBAR	badly	so-so	barely		
[]	[]	[]	[]	052	Mike Ramsay and Jim Barton
[]	[]	[]	[]	053	IBM
[]	[]	[]	[]	054	The Yellow Pages
[]	[]	[]	[]	055	Maurice Gatsonides
[]	[]	[]	[]	056	Overprotective parents
[]	[]	[]	[]	057	Jack Welch
[]	[]	[]	[]	058	Alex Rodriguez
[]	[]	[]	[]	059	The automatic-flush toilet inventor
[]	[]	[]	[]	060	Photoshop
[]	[]	[]	[]	061	R. Stanton Avery
[]	[]	[]	[]	062	Germaphobes
[]	[]	[]	[]	063	The U.S. Department of Agriculture
[]	[]	[]	[]	064	The imperial system of measurement
[]	[]	[]	[]	065	John DeLorean
[]	[]	[]	[]	066	Pope Siricius
[]	[]	[]	[]	067	Ken Lay and Jeff Skilling
[]	[]	[]	[]	068	Scott Boras and Drew Rosenhaus
[]	[]	[]	[]	069	Monica Lewinsky
[]	[]	[]	[]	070	Tyler Durden
[]	[]	[]	[]	071	Sony's Betamax
[]	[]	[]	[]	072	Car alarm users
[]	[]	[]	[]	073	Asbestos companies
[]	[]	[]	[]	074	Dr. Robert Atkins
[]	[]	[]	[]	075	Phil Gramm
[]	[]	[]	[]	076	*MLA Handbook*
[]	[]	[]	[]	077	Blue Star LSD warnings
[]	[]	[]	[]	078	The Food and Drug Administration
[]	[]	[]	[]	079	Ron Popeil
[]	[]	[]	[]	080	James Mack Jr.
[]	[]	[]	[]	081	Barbra Streisand
[]	[]	[]	[]	082	Edward Seymour
[]	[]	[]	[]	083	Thomas Hamilton
[]	[]	[]	[]	084	Dean Kamen
[]	[]	[]	[]	085	E85
[]	[]	[]	[]	086	General Motors
[]	[]	[]	[]	087	Michael John Anderson
[]	[]	[]	[]	088	Henry Phillips
[]	[]	[]	[]	089	Tian Wenhua
[]	[]	[]	[]	090	Walter Diemer
[]	[]	[]	[]	091	The United States
[]	[]	[]	[]	092	The New York Mercantile Exchange
[]	[]	[]	[]	093	The paparazzi
[]	[]	[]	[]	094	Los Angeles
[]	[]	[]	[]	095	MTV
[]	[]	[]	[]	096	Charles Darwin
[]	[]	[]	[]	097	Wal-Mart shoppers
[]	[]	[]	[]	098	Pamela and Gela of Juicy Couture
[]	[]	[]	[]	099	Scotland
[]	[]	[]	[]	100	Shawn Meneely
[]	[]	[]	[]	101	The apple

ABOUT THE AUTHOR

Matthew Vincent has a background in architecture and design and has worked on a number of projects ranging from high-end residential and civic projects to branding and product design. He currently works as a freelance designer/ideator at his start-up design company, Fluid Figment. He lives in Los Angeles with his wife, Mélanie, and their daughter, Téa.

don't forget to drink your ovaltine!